Better Beer & How to Brew It

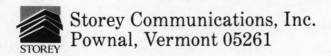

M. R. Reese

A Garden Way Publishing Book

Storey Communications, Inc.
Pownal, Vermont 05261

Photographs by Erik Borg
Illustrations by Nancy Anisfield

Printed in the United States by Courier Stoughton
Eleventh Printing, August 1990

Library of Congress Cataloging in Publication Data

Reese, M.R.
    Better beer and how to brew it.

    Includes index.
    1. Brewing.   2. Beer.   I. Title.
TP570.R37   641.8'73   81-7003
ISBN 0-88266-257-0   AACR2

 Contents

Acknowledgments

I am indebted to my neighbor, Betty McLernon, for her willing assistance with the book. I would also like to thank Mary Dunnigan, librarian, Fine Arts Library, University of Virginia, for research assistance. Finally, I would like to thank my daughter, Donna, for helping develop some of the illustrations, and my wife, Dottie, for tolerating these years of brewing experiments in her kitchen.

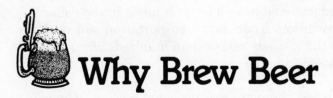# Why Brew Beer

"Make my own beer? Why should I?"

This I hear constantly—and usually from someone who has a commercial beer in hand, and who, five minutes ago, was either complaining about the high cost of that beer, or moaning that they just don't make beer like they used to.

And right there are hints as to why you should try making your own beer. Two reasons:

1. You'll save money.
2. You'll make a beer that tastes better.

Let's first explore how you can save money.

You'll need some equipment, but not much, and it's not very expensive.

And after that you'll pay only for the ingredients. Count on twenty to twenty-five cents for a twelve-ounce bottle. It can be a little more if your tastes are expensive, and you want only the most expensive ingredients.

But how can you expect to make, at home, beer for less money than a big manufacturer can make it? The reason is that he has a lot of expenses that you won't have. Here are some of them.

1

1. Taxes. Not a cent for you. A varying amount is paid by the big company, depending on what each state thinks the consumer will stand still for.

2. Advertising. Advertising is the last thing you want to do if you're brewing your own. You'll get enough drop-in trade of neighbors and relatives when they recognize you're making a superior product—and have a lot of it down in the cellar.

3. Transportation. Your only transportation will be from the cellar to the kitchen, rather than hundreds of miles from brewery to store to home.

As you can see, there are reasons, good reasons, why commercial beer costs as much as it does today. You can agree with this, but that doesn't mean you have to pay the price. Not when you can make beer for bargain prices and avoid the expenses that don't improve the taste of the beer one bit.

Better Beer

But will the beer you make be as good as commercial beer? This question is usually asked by those who have been drinking beer for many a year. They remember home brew as a yeasty, strong, dark drink that occasionally popped corks or shattered bottles, and just plain didn't taste all that good. A lot of that was made in Prohibition days, when malt extract was dissolved in water in an open crock, and sugar, a few potato peels, and raisins were added, and a cake of baker's yeast was floated on a piece of toast. This was bottled after fermenting for a few days, then was drunk quickly, before the bottles began to explode.

Beer such as that is made today only by the rankest of amateurs, and they deserve every headache they brew up for themselves. Those amateurs aren't taking advantage of the vastly superior ingredients available today. Nor are they using the far more sophisticated methods that have been devised, methods no more difficult than those of yesterday, but certainly offering a better beer. The difference between the fresh, rich taste of home-brewed beer as compared to commercial beer's flavor is often compared to the difference between fresh home-baked bread and the store-bought variety.

There's yet another reason for brewing beer. A growing number of people are finding it a satisfying and creative hobby. They become so interested in the art and science of brewing that they continually expand their brewing skills and knowledge, and experiment with different materials, recipes, and methods.

This book is written for both the beginner and the advanced hobbyist.

Two Approaches

The first section describes the basic processes and procedures for brewing good quality beers from malt extracts. You may be perfectly satisfied to limit your efforts to these straightforward procedures.

If you wish to develop your brewing skills further and join the ranks of the more advanced brewers, I urge you to try the procedures described in the second section. They are a little more time-consuming but they are not difficult.

I have been observing the development of home brewing in the United States, Canada, and England since 1970. I have watched ideas, equipment, and ingredients being imported. When I first began watching, make no mistake about it, the English were far ahead of us. That's true no longer. We've caught up, and now we're developing our own approaches to beer quality, and we can hold our home beer up to anyone's.

Takes Little Time

Perhaps you are still a bit wary about trying to brew beer. You're ready to agree that you can save money this way, and the beer itself may be better. But, you tell yourself, there must be a hitch. Is it because it's so much work that no one would put in all of those hours, just for five gallons of beer?

Let me promise you this—you'll be surprised how easy it is from the first time you try. And, even better, you'll be delighted when you find how much you enjoy experimenting and tasting and sharing a big, cold bottle of your best with a friend.

How much time does it take?

This book describes two basic methods for making beer. One is simple, and the other is slightly more complicated so that you have a bit more control over the resulting beer.

For the person in a hurry—the shorter, easier method.

This breaks down into mixing the various ingredients. Let's give that an hour, and that's time enough to reread the instructions in this book.

The five-gallon mixture now sits for from five to seven days, foaming as it ferments, which means the sugar in the mixture is converted into alcohol and carbon dioxide.

So, about a week later, you will add a bit of sugar to the mixture, then bottle it in bottles you've scrubbed. Give yourself two hours for all of this.

Result: Five gallons of beer for three hours of work.

Waiting

And now for the most difficult part of beer-making. There it is in the bottle. How does it taste? Will it have too much gas in it, or will it be flat? For the answers to those questions, you must wait four to six weeks while the beer ages. It's hard to do.

We believe no one has ever waited four weeks before tasting a bottle of the first batch of beer. If you succumb to temptation, remember that the last bottle of that batch will probably taste the best, since it's had a chance to age longer.

One final thought, before we get down to brewing. Although I have spent five years in experimenting with various ways to make beer, I still don't believe there's one single *best* method. There are alternate approaches and methods. In this book I've tried to offer you these alternatives so that you can try them, and see which ones you prefer. In that way you may find a method that suits you best, and results in the exact beer you want. On the other hand, there are steps that I believe shouldn't be changed if you want a quality beer. In these cases I've tried to emphasize those steps, so that you won't be disappointed in the results from the first batch of beer that you brew.

Understanding Beer

In this book we'll use the term beer as any alcoholic beverage of up to about 6 percent alcohol which is fermented from water, malt, and hops. This includes lagers, ales, steam beers, and stouts. We'll explain the difference between those later, but for now let us explore the basic process common to the production of all beers.

That basic process is fermentation. Fermentation is the breaking down of sugars into alcohol and carbon dioxide gas. This is done by microscopic organisms called yeast. For the yeast to do this, the solution must have certain nutrients, particularly nitrogen and phosphorus. During fermentation, about half the sugar is converted to alcohol, and the other half is converted to carbon dioxide gas which bubbles to the surface and escapes.

A solution of sugar, nutrients, yeast, and water would provide an alcoholic liquid, but not a very appealing one for drinking.

So, to make beer, we must add some other ingredients that will give it such pleasing characteristics as good flavor, aroma, color, and body. Additionally, if we wish the beer to be carbonated, and have a head when we pour it, we must retain a part of that carbon dioxide gas.

7

Let's consider the two ingredients that will give beer its taste, aroma, color, and body.

Malt

The first of these is *malt*. Malt is made from barley, a grain. The barley is soaked in water, allowed to sprout, then the sprouts are dried in a kiln. Converting the barley to malt in this manner allows dormant enzymes in the barley to develop. These enzymes are capable of doing some very specific tasks. One of those tasks is to convert starches into sugar, which is a process called *mashing*.

Malting changes the grain in other ways. The hard, starchy grain becomes sweeter, with a slightly withered and softened husk.

BREWING AND THE LAW

Both state and federal laws cover the brewing of beer.

State laws vary widely, with some of them prohibiting home brewing. Check on the law in your state by calling police or state or county prosecutors.

For many years the Internal Revenue Service specified that a home brewer must pay an alcoholic beverage tax, but there was little effort made to collect that tax.

Such uncertainty has been eliminated now. On February 1, 1979 Congress passed the Cranston Bill. This specifically permits the brewing of up to 100 gallons of beer per year in a one-adult household, and the brewing of up to 200 gallons per year in households of two or more persons aged eighteen or older.

Hops

The second ingredient added to flavor the beer is *hops*. Hops are the dried female flowers of the hop plant, a vine with the scientific name of *Humulus lupulus.* The hop flower contains acids and oils that provide a degree of bitterness, to offset the sweetness of the malt, plus a tangy flavor and aroma to the beer. In order to get those characteristics into the beer, the hops are boiled with the malt extract, a process called *hopping.*

When we combine water, malt, and hops we have a sugary, bittersweet liquid which is called *wort* (and pronounced wert). If we add yeast to it, it will ferment into beer.

Malt Extracts

Before you throw up your hands at the prospect of trying to do all of these steps, let me explain that you have to do only one of them to brew your own beer. You can buy commercially prepared *malt extracts,* which take care of the malting, mashing, and hopping steps for us, and thus we have a product which greatly simplifies beer making.

Essentially, these malt extracts are made by concentrating commercial worts into heavy syrup or powdered form.

The home brewer only needs to add water to the extract to make up the wort. He then adds yeast, which will ferment the wort into beer.

Getting a Head

The final step will be to carbonate the beer to give it that lively, zesty character and a nice foamy head. In commercial brewing the general practice is to capture a portion of the carbon dioxide gas generated during fermentation and add it back to the finished beer when the beer is bottled.

In home brewing it's done a bit differently. A small amount of *priming* sugar is added to the beer at bottling time. This restarts the fermentation process by which the sugar is converted to alcohol and carbon dioxide, and the carbon dioxide is captured in the capped bottle.

If you look back over the material you've just read, you'll see that making beer at home need not be difficult, thanks to the malt extracts that are on the market today that provide you with a concentrate to which you need only add yeast and water.

Commercial beers vary in taste and other qualities because of variations in malting, mashing, and hopping. Similarly, you can buy different malt extracts to make a wide variety of beers. Thus, by finding an extract that exactly suits your taste, and altering the process in subtle ways to be explained, you can brew a beer exactly to your own personal taste.

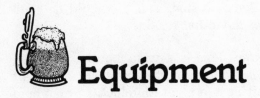 # Equipment

Here's a list of the equipment you will need for brewing. You'll probably have some of the items in your kitchen; others can be purchased from a winemaking and brewing supply store. These are often listed in the Yellow Pages under winemaking.

You'll note that the list is for both single-stage and two-stage brewing with different equipment required only in the fermenting step. The two methods will be explained.

Boiling pot, 2–6 gallons
Single-stage fermenter, 7–8 gallons
 (for single-stage method)
Primary fermenter, 7–8 gallons
 (for two-stage method)
Secondary fermenter, 5 gallons
 (for two-stage method)
Fermentation lock
 (with rubber stopper for two-stage method)

Siphon
Hydrometer
Bottles, enough to hold 5 gallons
Bottle brush
Bottle capper
Bottle caps
Wooden spoon, long-handled
Measuring spoons
Strainer
Kitchen scales
Measuring cup
Thermometer

Let's take a closer look at some of the equipment.

Boiling pot. This is used for mixing the ingredients and boiling the wort. It should have a capacity of at least two gallons. A larger pot of up to six gallons is preferred. A large enameled canning kettle is fine if it is not chipped on the inside. A stainless steel kettle is fine, also. It should be completely free of grease or any other residue.

Single-stage fermenter. This is a wide-mouth container, made of a plastic that is food-grade. It must have an airtight lid and a place for inserting a fermentation lock. It must hold seven or eight gallons, since the beer will form a heavy head during the first stages of fermentation.

Primary fermenter. A good quality (preferably food-grade) plastic container of seven to eight gallons capacity. A better-grade plastic garbage container is suitable. White is the preferred color. You should neutralize the plastic container before using by washing it with bicarbonate of soda and water, then rinsing it. A stone crock can also be used, but it will be heavy and cumbersome. Make certain your crock does not have a lead glaze, which could be toxic. With either one you will need a sheet of plastic to cover the top and thus avoid contamination.

Secondary fermenter. The ideal item for this is a five-gallon water bottle, or carboy. A fermentation lock can be fitted to the bottle by inserting a one-hole rubber stopper in the mouth of the carboy. Most five-gallon water bottles take either a number 6½ or 7 rubber stopper. An alternate and less acceptable container is a five-gallon polyethylene plastic bottle.

Fermentation lock. This lock is placed in the top of the container during fermentation. It permits the carbon dioxide generated during fermentation to escape from the container, but keeps air from entering the container. There are several models, all designed with one or more elbows containing water, so that the gas can bubble up through the water. This enables you to monitor the fermentation activity. The lock of course must be securely sealed to the fermenter so that there are no air leaks.

Siphon. After the mixing of the wort, any further movement of the liquid is done through a siphon, rather than by pouring. In this way, it is possible to lessen exposure to air, and to avoid transfer of any settlings. The simplest form of siphon is a six-foot piece of ⅜-inch plastic tubing. Two accessories will make siphoning much more efficient. One is a racking tube, which is a rigid plastic tube. It fits into one end of the flexible tubing and is placed in the container from which the beer is being siphoned. The racking tube can be attached to a dowel in such a way that the beer is not siphoned from the bottom of the container, to avoid siphoning settlings. The second item is a siphon clamp. It is made of spring steel or nylon and fits over the other end of the flexible tubing. This allows the flow to be easily started and stopped when filling bottles.

Hydrometer. This is a measuring device you will need to have and to understand, since the success of your beer depends in part on proper use of it. The hydrometer will tell you when the beer has fermented down to the bottling point, that is, when all the sugars have been converted to alcohol and carbon dioxide.

The hydrometer is a simple instrument in that it measures the density of a liquid as compared to the density of pure water. This measurement is expressed as the specific gravity of the liquid, the specific gravity of water being 1.000. Thus when the hydrometer is floated in a tube of water, the instrument should sink to where the reading of the figures at the waterline is very close to 1.000. Most hydrometers are marked so that all of the figures of the reading are not shown. Thus, 1.050 may be shown as 50.

Most hydrometers are calibrated to measure correctly

when the liquid is at 60° F. If the temperature of the liquid is ten or more degrees away from 60°, a correction in the reading must be made. The accompanying graph gives temperature corrections.

A good hydrometer should measure from 1.000 or below to 1.100. It should be at least nine inches long to be sufficiently accurate. You will need a test tube or testing jar nine or more inches in length to hold the liquid being measured.

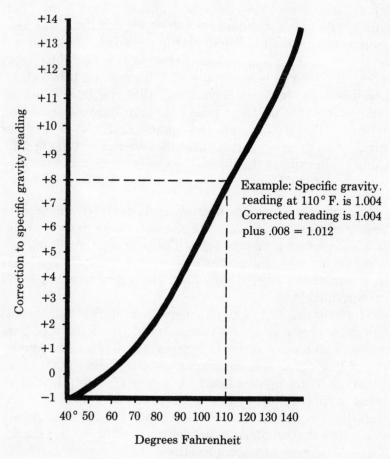

Example: Specific gravity reading at 110° F. is 1.004 Corrected reading is 1.004 plus .008 = 1.012

Degrees Fahrenheit

Temperature corrections for hydrometer readings.

In using the hydrometer, remember that a sugar solution is heavier than water, and thus the hydrometer will float higher in it. As the sugar is converted to alcohol, the hydrometer will sink lower and lower.

You will use the hydrometer to measure the starting gravity of the wort, and the gravity of the beer at the end of fermentation.

The starting gravity is simply a measurement of the total amount of solids that are dissolved in the wort. Most of them are sugars, but there is also a small amount of non-fermentable solids, dextrins, and protein materials. These non-fermentable solids will of course remain in the beer after fermentation, and thus you can expect a reading slightly above 1.000 in the finished beer. How much above this reading it will be depends on the various recipes and malts used.

For this reason the recipe should give an indication of the expected terminal gravity, or when the beer is ready to be bottled, with all sugar converted to alcohol. A typical terminal gravity reading is 1.004. This means that the hydrometer reading should be 1.004 or below before the beer is ready to be primed and bottled. A typical starting gravity would be about 1.040, which is the hydrometer reading of the wort before fermentation.

If hydrometer readings were taken each day after fermentation starts, the reading would drop each day until the terminal gravity of 1.004 were reached. Typically this would take from five to seven days. It isn't necessary to take the reading until close to the end of the anticipated fermentation period.

How to Read It

Reading the hydrometer is simple if you avoid two possible errors.

1. Small bubbles may adhere to the body of the hydrometer and hold it higher in the liquid, giving a false reading. This

won't happen if you place the hydrometer in the liquid, then spin it with your thumb and index finger, dislodging the bubbles.

2. You read it incorrectly because of the meniscus effect. You will notice that the liquid tends to creep up a bit along the side of the floating hydrometer. Read across the level of the liquid, not at the height of where it crept up on the hydrometer.

Bottles. Have enough to hold five gallons of beer. Any recappable bottle will do, however the best choice is the standard twelve-ounce green or brown glass returnable beer bottle or the American champagne bottle. You will need forty-eight or fifty of the smaller bottles; twenty-four or twenty-five of the larger ones. Discard any that are cracked or chipped.

Bottle brush. A nylon bristle brush with a handle long enough to reach the bottoms of the bottles used.

Bottle capper. There are several models. A hammer capper (which is struck with a hammer to tighten the cap around the top of the bottle) is inexpensive but more difficult than the others to use effectively. A hand lever capper is more expensive, easier to use, but in some models is limited to use on the standard long neck twelve-ounce bottle. The bench capper is best, most expensive (about $30), fastest to use, and is adjustable to any height bottle.

Bottle caps. These are standard crown caps and are usually sold in boxes of one gross.

Thermometer. The thermometer must be a model to measure the temperature of a liquid. A dairy-type model measuring up to 200° F. is fine.

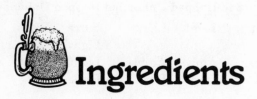 Ingredients

We're almost ready to begin brewing beer. But first—a few words on ingredients. Remember that not all of these will be used in every recipe. In the chapter on Understanding Beer we looked briefly at a few of the ingredients. Let's take a closer look at those and a few others.

Malt. When you buy malt for the first time, be prepared for a confusing array of products. Remember, first, that in the first recipes in this book you will be using *malt extract,* in which all of the work of converting the barley to a form ready for use in beer has been done for you.

There are light and dark types of malt extracts, as well as extracts that are hopped and unhopped. And there will be a variation among brands as to color, flavor, and hop content. Different brands come in different sizes, too. Typical sizes for canned malt syrups are 2, 2.2, 2.5, 3, 3.3, and 3.5 pounds.

The dried malt extracts, which are in powdered form and called dry malt, are usually sold by the pound and are often packaged in three-pound bags. These are always unhopped.

The accompanying table shows the wide variety of malt extracts available, and this of course is only a sample of what is on the market.

TYPICAL MALT EXTRACTS (SYRUPS)

	John Bull		Munton & Fison		Canadiana	
Origin	England		England		Canada	
Package Size	3.3 lb		3.5 lb		2.5 lb	
Types	**Hopped**	**Unhopped**	**Hopped**	**Unhopped**	**Hopped**	**Unhopped**
	Light	Light	Light	Light	Extra-Light[1]	Extra-Light[1]
	Amber	Amber	Amber	Amber	Light	Light
	Dark	Dark	Dark	Dark	Dark	Dark

	Edme		Superbrau[2]	
Orgin	England		USA	
Package Size	3.5 lb		5.1 lb	
Types	**Hopped**	**Unhopped**	**Hopped**	**Unhopped**
	Light	Light	Light	Light
	Dark	Dark	Amber	Amber
	—	—	Dark	Dark

1. Contains part corn syrup.
2. Superbrau products are a premixed ingredient pack containing malt extract and corn syrup. The unhopped pack may be used in the Basic Beer recipe in place of malt extract and corn sugar. The product is labeled Pilsener, Octoberfest, and Bock for light, amber, and dark respectively.

Each recipe gives a recommendation on the type and amount of malt extract to be used. By referring to the table, you can select an appropriate malt for each recipe. As you experiment, you will find those that are your favorites.

Dried hops. Hops will add a tangy flavor and aroma to your beer. Even when hopped malt extracts are used, the quality of the beer, and particularly its aroma, can be improved by boiling a small amount of hops in the wort for five to fifteen minutes. This procedure can easily be extended to complete hopping of worts made from unhopped malt extracts.

But don't think that very good beers can't be made from hopped malt extracts without the use of dried hops. Many brewers are content to use the hopped malt extracts alone.

Choice of hops

The choice of hop variety depends on the type of beer you're brewing as well as your own personal preference. The different varieties have differing degrees of bitterness and aroma.

The accompanying table gives some indications of the characteristics and use of some of the more commonly available hop varieties.

The information is somewhat arbitrary, but it will provide some insight into the variations in hops. The table shows, for example, that Brewer's Gold is one of the strongest hop varieties in bitterness and aroma. This variety would only be used in making beers with a high degree of bitterness and relatively strong flavor such as a heavy dark stout.

RELATIVE CHARACTERISTICS
OF HOP VARIETIES

Variety	Relative Bitterness	Relative Aromatics	Use
Brewer's Gold	1.0	2.5	Flavoring
Cluster	0.9	1.0	Flavoring
Cascade	0.6	1.5	Flavoring & finishing
Hallertauer	0.6	1.0	Flavoring & finishing
Fuggles	0.5	1.0	Flavoring & finishing
Kent	0.5	1.0	Finishing

The higher numbers indicate greater strength.

The table does not give any indication of relative quality since this is a very subjective judgment. In my opinion, the three best varieties for quality beers are Hallertauer, Cascade, and Fuggles.

Yeast. Yeast is a single-celled organism belonging to the fungus family. There are many varieties of yeast, even including so-called "wild" yeast floating in the air around us. Some are well suited for specific uses, such as for making bread, for wine, or for beer.

There are two types of yeast used in brewing beer.

1. Top-fermenting yeast (Saccharomyces cerevisiae) has the same scientific name as the yeast used for baking bread, but the two strains are different. This yeast is used for making ales and stouts. The name "top-fermenting" is appropriate, since fermentation takes place on the top of the wort when this yeast is used.

2. Bottom-fermenting yeast (Saccharomyces carlsbergensis) is used to make lager and steam beers.

A good beer yeast will start fermenting quickly, impart good flavor to the beer, and settle out completely to produce brilliant clarity in the beer.

Initially you will have to depend on your supplier to make recommendations on the best yeast type. Eventually you will develop your own preferences from experience.

Don't use baker's yeast

Whatever you do, don't spoil a good batch of beer by using baker's yeast. Bread yeast doesn't settle out properly and tends to give the beer a musty flavor and aroma.

And don't try a sample of brewer's yeast from that you bought at the health-food store to add vitamins to your diet. Nothing will happen if you do. The yeast bought for that purpose is no longer alive.

Water. In terms of volume, water is the most important in-gredient in beer. Fully 90 percent of beer is water. That makes it important enough to make certain your supply is good.

Water must be palatable and free of contamination. If it is not palatable, the taste of the beer will be the same. If it is contaminated, such as with a high bacterial count, it may be necessary to sterilize it by boiling. Untreated water that is contaminated can be the cause of souring of the beer. If your water supply is from a well or spring and is untreated it is a good idea to boil it and not take chances.

Hard and soft water

The degree of hardness of water is also a factor in the taste of beer. Beers brewed from soft water tend to be milder in flavor than those made from hard water. This degree of hard-ness is determined by the amount of mineral elements dis-solved in it. The particular types of minerals in the water will also affect the character of the beer.

Most public water supplies in the United States have rela-tively soft water. Because of this, many beer recipes call for the addition of water hardeners such as gypsum, table salt, or special water treatments such as Burton salts. In many cases such water treatment is optional. Experimenting will deter-mine which water treatment may be needed for your special case. Some brewers find it worthwhile to search out special sources of water for their brews, but generally this is not nec-essary.

Sugar. Many recipes call for the use of sugar, and it is used to raise the level of the alcohol in the finished product. "All-malt" beers are made without sugar and are heavier in body and fuller in flavor than those that use sugar. Sugar is used to lighten beer or to make it at less cost, since sugar is less ex-pensive than malt.

The sugar in malt is called malt sugar or maltose.

If sugar is to be added, the best one to use is dextrose, or corn sugar, rather than sucrose, or cane sugar, the type found in sugar bowls. Corn sugar is more readily fermented than household sugar and is not so inclined to produce a "cidery" tasting beer.

Even corn sugar should not be used in excessive amounts, or the quality of the beer will suffer. As a general rule, the ratio of malt to sugar should be no less than about two to one. This means that there should be at least two parts of malt to one part of sugar.

Of the other sugars sometimes called for in beer recipes, milk sugar or lactose is sometimes used in stouts, and molasses, or brown sugar, sometimes is added to flavor the dark ales. I do not recommend the use of these ingredients.

Additives in Brewing

Several additives are used by some brewers. They perform such functions as anti-oxidation, improving head retention, and clarifying the beer. These additives are usually optional, used at the discretion of the brewer.

Finings. Finings, or fining agents, are added to beer to assist in clarification. Most commercially available fining agents are gelatin products which are dissolved in a small amount of hot water and mixed with the beer at priming or when the beer is transferred to a secondary fermenter. Their use in single-stage fermentation, when all fermentation is carried out in one container, is not practical unless the beer is primed in bulk. Otherwise the finings would stir up the yeast sediment. Beers that are properly made will normally develop brilliant clarity without the use of finings.

Anti-oxidants. Anti-oxidants are used to protect the beer from the effects of oxygen which may be absorbed in the beer during siphoning or at some other time. Ascorbic acid, or vitamin C, is commonly used, and added to the beer at priming and bottling. It is available in powder form and is used at the rate of one-half to one teaspoon per five-gallon batch of beer.

Heading liquid. Heading liquid affects the surface tension of the beer in such a way as to improve the retention of the head. It also seems to produce a thicker, creamier head on beers that are properly carbonated. If you like lots of head, use a half-teaspoon of heading liquid per five gallons of beer. Heading compounds in dry form are difficult to use. Use liquids obtainable at stores handling materials for making wines and beer.

Spruce essence. This is very strongly flavored and must be used at a rate of no more than a quarter- or half-teaspoon per five gallons of beer. Spruce essence is of value to the experienced brewer in duplicating the character of certain European lagers.

Yeast nutrient. To remain healthy and carry out the fermentation, yeast must have available a sufficient supply of nutrients. The principal ones required are phosphorus and nitrogen. Several commercial formulations are available which provide additional nutrients. The most common of these is a white powder called diammonium phosphate. If a good recipe is used, one that has sufficient malt content, additional nutrients are not needed since they are supplied by the malt.

VARIETIES

Here are the four basic beer varieties you will make with the recipes to follow. You'll note they differ as to the methods of using a variety of ingredients, and that fermentation temperatures differ.

Lagers. Lager beers are produced by fermenting with a bottom-fermenting, or lager, yeast at low temperatures. Commercial brewers use fermentation temperatures in the range of 50° F. or below. The fermentation period at these temperatures is extended because the yeast is not as active and thus it takes longer to use up all of the sugars in the wort. The home brewer may produce true lagers by using a refrigerator or other means of maintaining these cool temperatures. In practice, most home brewers are satisfied to ferment their lagers in the range of 55–70° F. Lagers are either light or dark, and are characterized by fairly low alcohol and hop content, and a crisp, dry flavor.

Ales. Commercial ales are fermented with top-fermenting yeasts in the temperature range of 55–65° F. They typically have higher alcohol and hop contents than lagers. Ales tend to have a sharper, more robust flavor than lagers. They range in color from light to dark. Good home-brewed ales may be made at temperatures up to 70–75° F.

Steam Beers. Very few commercial steam beers are being produced. Probably the most famous is Anchor Steam Beer, which is brewed in San Francisco. Technically, steam beer is brewed with a bottom-fermenting, or lager, yeast in the temperature range of 60–65° F. Probably most home-brewed beers could be classed as steam beers because they are mostly fermented with bottom-fermenting yeast at temperatures ranging from 60 to 75° F.

24

Stouts. Stouts are very heavy, very dark beers brewed from top-fermenting yeasts. They are generally highly hopped beers. The high hop content is balanced by the use of large amounts of malt, including some dark malts, whose full flavors offset the bitterness of the hops. Stouts can range in flavor from dry to fairly sweet.

You will find many variations among these varieties of beers, depending on the brewer. You will also find many recipes for each of them. The recipes provided in this book are fairly basic ones. You can modify them to suit your fancy.

The home brewer can obtain good results at temperatures up to 75° F. Temperatures higher than this encourage the development of undesirable ferments that affect quality and taste. In general, the best quality beers are made at lower, rather than higher temperatures.

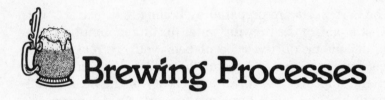# Brewing Processes

Let's take a quick look at the various processes used in making beer so that you will have a broad picture of the methods before you get into the specific how-to of the next chapter.

The processes we describe have two aims.

One of them is to enable you to make a satisfactory beer on the first try.

The second is to show you ways to vary your procedures so that you can improve your beer and finally make a beer exactly to your liking.

Such procedures haven't always been used in home brewing in this country. In the Prohibition days, hop-flavored malt extract and sugar were mixed in water, then yeast was added. This mixture was allowed to ferment in an open container such as a stone crock. The result was sometimes drinkable, but more often the home brew was of poor quality.

With the processes described in this book, you should be able to make high quality beers that equal or surpass the best commercial beers you have tasted.

The following are the basic steps in brewing beer:

1. *Preparing the wort.* This involves mixing the malt extract, hops, and sometimes sugar, in the water.

Remember three points in this step.

a. Use ingredients of good quality.

b. Mix the ingredients in the proportions called for in the recipe for the type of beer you are making.

c. Prepare the mixture in such a way as to prevent contamination by various spoilage organisms that could ruin the beer.

The best worts are prepared by boiling malt extracts with at least a part of the brewing water for fifteen minutes to one hour depending on the type of beer you are making. The longer boiling period is for dark beers. Boiling sterilizes the wort and improves the flavor and clarity of the beer. Ideally you will boil the full volume of the wort. As a compromise, you can boil only one or two gallons with the malt extract, then make up the remaining volume of a five-gallon batch by adding water.

As you get more experience with making beer you will want to try adding dried hops to the wort. You will learn that beer quality, and particularly aroma, are improved if a small amount of hops is added to the wort and boiled for five to fifteen minutes. This method can be used even with hopped malt extracts.

2. *Fermentation.* This step involves adding yeast, then permitting the yeast to work under ideal conditions.

The wort, which has boiled, is allowed to cool to about 75 to 80° F. Then the correct yeast is added. The yeast begins to multiply rapidly and within twenty-four hours the fermentation will begin to erupt into vigorous bubbling, with the formation of a layer of foam on the surface of the liquid. The foam, or head, is caused by the carbon dioxide gas, which is generated by the breakdown of the sugars by the yeast.

The fermentation, or conversion of the sugars into alcohol, typically takes about five to seven days, at room temperature. The foam layer lasts for two to three days and then subsides as the fermentation approaches the end.

3. *Priming and bottling.* This step involves adding a small quantity of sugar (priming), then siphoning the beer into the bottles, and capping them.

The fermentation is complete. The sugar has been converted into alcohol and carbon dioxide gas, and the gas has escaped. It's time to prime the beer and bottle it.

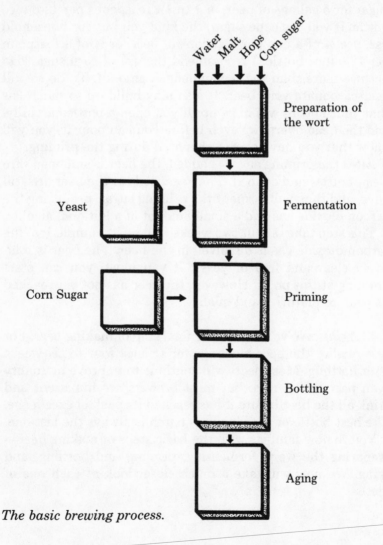

The basic brewing process.

Priming involves adding just the right amount of sugar to the beer. When it ferments in the bottle, it will produce the correct amount of carbonation. To make certain the beer is ready for priming, you'll be checking it with your hydrometer. More about this later.

Most recipes call for adding about 1 to 1¼ cups of corn sugar for 5 gallons of beer, or 1 to 1¼ teaspoons per 12-ounce bottle. If you use cane sugar, the kind you buy for household use, use ¾ of a cup per 5 gallons of beer, or ¾ of a teaspoon per 12-ounce bottle. I recommend the use of corn sugar. Do not use more than the recommended amount. To do so will over-carbonate your beer. It also may build up so much gas that your bottles will blow up. If you open a bottle carefully, and the head overflows even before you can pour it, you will know that you have over-carbonated during the priming.

After the priming sugar is added, the beer is siphoned into clean bottles and capped. The yeast cells in the beer are still alive, and they will ferment the priming sugar, producing the carbon dioxide gas and a small amount of additional alcohol.

This step takes about two weeks, and on its completion, the carbon dioxide gas is dissolved in the beer. The beer is relatively clear and free of yeast. If you must, you can start drinking at this point. However, the beer has not yet reached its peak of maturity and quality.

4. *Aging.* We've reached the final step of making beer. For best quality the beer must age for at least four to six weeks after bottling. Most beers will continue to improve in quality even past this period, but most brewers are impatient and drink all the beer before it has reached its peak of excellence. The best bottle of beer in every batch is always the last one.

You're now familiar with the basic steps of making beer—preparing the wort, fermenting, priming and bottling, and aging. We now will take a much closer look at each one of these.

Brewing with Malt Extracts

We've discussed ingredients, equipment, and the basics of brewing. We're ready to begin brewing.

You'll see in these directions that you have a choice of two methods for fermenting beer. These are called the single-stage and the two-stage methods.

In the first, fermentation is completed in a single container.

In the second, the fermentation is started in one container, then, after two or three days, the liquid is transferred to a second container.

There are advantages to both systems, and your choice may depend on the equipment you have.

The advantages of the single-stage method are:

1. It requires less equipment. You need one container rather than two.

2. It takes less of your time. One step, the transfer of the liquid from one container to another, is eliminated.

3. It eliminates some handling of the beer, with the danger of more exposure of the liquid to the air.

The advantages of the two-stage method:

1. There's less exposure of the beer to air during the second step, when fermentation is slower. The chance of contact

with air is less because the beer is up into the neck of the car-boy, leaving little area for possible exposure.

2. The beer is moved off the sediment, thus if the beer is siphoned carefully, leaving the sediment behind, the opportunity for this to get into the bottles is eliminated.

I prefer the single-stage method, but will explain both.

Regardless of which method is used, one requirement is of extreme importance: the fermenting wort must be given maximum protection from exposure to air. The reason for this is that various organisms, primarily bacteria, which can cause spoilage of the beer, must have air to grow. Conversely, beer yeasts do not require air to carry out their task of fermentation. By shutting out the air from the fermenting beer, activity by these undesirable organisms can be prevented.

In both methods, the air is excluded from the fermenting wort by using a simple device called a fermentation lock, described earlier.

Sanitation

Good sanitation, or just plain cleanliness, is important through the procedure of brewing, since it is so closely linked with the production of a beer of the finest taste. Bottles and all containers and other equipment that come in contact with the beer must be as free of foreign matter and undesirable organisms as possible.

This does not mean that we have to do our brewing in a sterile environment and wear a surgical mask. Good kitchen sanitation is the general rule. Use of a sterilizing agent is good insurance.

There are several methods of sterilizing the bottles and equipment.

Probably the best sterilizing agent is sulfur dioxide. This is

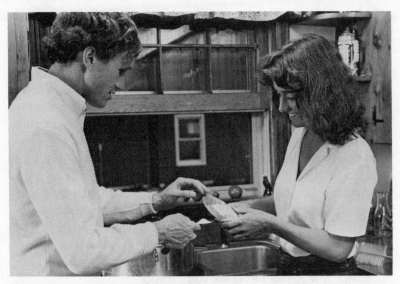

Fred and Andrea add sterilizing agent to water, preparing to wash bottles and all brewing equipment.

A good nylon brush, such as this one, quickly cleans inside of bottles. Next step is to rinse with hot water and drain.

easily produced by dissolving either potassium or sodium bi-sulfite (or metabisulfite) in water. Make this sterilizing solution by adding two teaspoons of the chemical to each quart of water. Adding a pinch of citric acid will enhance the release of the sulfur dioxide. Two quarts of the solution is ample for each sterilizing job. Bathe the equipment in the solution, leave it in the solution for a few minutes, then rinse thoroughly with hot water.

Another sterilizing agent that is satisfactory is common household chlorine bleach. You can make a sterilizing solution from this by mixing two tablespoons of bleach in a half-gallon of water. The only problem with chlorine bleach is that it is a little more difficult to rinse off than the sulfite solution. If you use the bleach solution, take care to rinse several times with hot water to remove all traces of the bleach, which could adversely affect the flavor of your beer.

If you have an automatic dishwasher and hot tap water, using them is the easiest way to sterilize bottles. Clean the bottles first with hot water and a brush, then place them upside down on the bottom rack of the washer and run them through the hot rinse and dry cycle. The bottles will come out dry and ready for priming and filling.

You will notice that in all of this discussion, I have not suggested using what you would ordinarily use for such work—common soap or detergents and water. These should be avoided as they are difficult to rinse out and any residue will be detrimental to the taste of the beer.

If your equipment or bottles are very dirty, use washing soda. That is a laundry powder that can be bought in most supermarkets. It is used for washing by making a mild solution of the powder mixed with hot water—about two teaspoons of powder per gallon of water.

If you use a good brush, this solution will remove stains and other foreign matter from equipment and bottles. After washing with this solution, rinse the equipment or bottles with hot water and drain them.

Preparing the Wort

First, here is the method for preparing the wort when you are using hopped malt extracts and are not using additional hops.

Place at least one gallon of water in the boiling pot. It is better to use two or more gallons if you have a large enough pot. Bring the water to a boil. Remove the pot from the heat and dissolve the malt extract in the water by stirring thoroughly. Malt syrups are more easily removed from the can if the can is warmed in hot water for a few minutes. Put the pot back on the heat and again bring to a boil.

Be sure not to fill the pot too full. The liquid will froth up when boiling and may overflow.

Continue a good rolling boil for fifteen or twenty minutes if you are making a light beer. If you are making a dark beer,

Andrea pours warmed can of malt into three gallons of boiling water. Next she will put kettle back on heat.

boil for as much as an hour. This is something you can experiment with, since you may find that you like the beer made from a wort that has been boiled longer, or you may conclude you can make a good dark beer by using the shorter boiling time.

While the wort is boiling, put any other ingredients such as the corn sugar, BUT NOT THE YEAST, in the single-stage fermenter, *or the primary fermenter if you are using the two-stage method.* When the boiling is complete, pour the hot liquid from the pot onto the other ingredients in the fermenter, and stir to mix thoroughly.

Top up the mixture with water to a total volume of five gallons, and stir again.

Put the lid of the single-stage fermenter in place and set aside to cool. The fermentation lock should be in place.

If you are using the two-stage method, cover the primary fermenter with a plastic sheet, then hold it in place with a string tied around the fermenter.

With either fermenter, you'll find it easier to fill to a total of five gallons if you measure one-gallon increments in advance, and mark them with a dab of fingernail polish on the outside of the container.

Cool the Wort

With both methods, cool the wort as rapidly as possible to 75–80° F. The wort is most vulnerable to the occurrence of "off" ferments by bacteria during this cooling period. These undesirable ferments can give the beer a sourish or cidery taste. Placing the fermenter in an ice water bath or in a refrigerator is a good idea if you have the facilities for doing so.

Use a good thermometer to measure the temperature of the wort and make certain it is in the 75–80° F. range. Much cooler and the yeast will not go to work as it should; if the wort is too hot, it will kill the yeast.

She carefully measures the amount of corn sugar called for in the recipe, and adds it to the boiling wort.

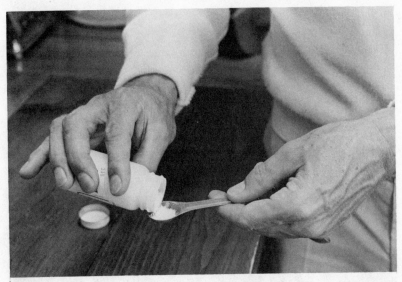

Fred measures the gypsum, which he will add to the boiling wort, along with all other ingredients except the yeast.

Andrea stirs boiling wort. She is timing this to give it the time called for in the recipe.

Fred adds tap water to the container, to bring the total volume to five gallons, as marked on the side of the container.

If the single-stage fermenter is being used, the lid is placed on it, and the fermentation lock is put in place.

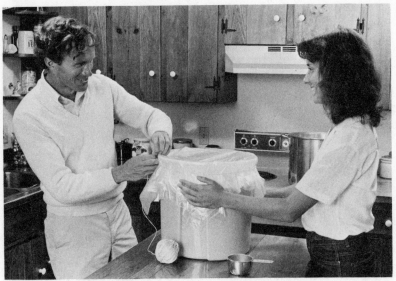

Fred and Andrea cover the primary fermenter with a plastic sheet, held in place with a piece of string.

Hopping the Wort

If you use a recipe that calls for hopping the wort, that step is taken when the mix is boiled.

There are two phases to hopping beer. These are referred to as flavoring and finishing. The purpose of the flavoring phase is to extract the desired tangy flavor from the hops and to add a degree of bitterness to the beer. The amount of flavor and bitterness depends on a combination of the variety of hop used, the amount of hops used, and the total boiling time. The purpose of the finishing phase is to add hop aroma to the beer with a minimum of additional flavor and bitterness.

To flavor the beer, you will boil larger amounts of hops with the malt for longer periods of time, while the finishing phase calls for smaller amounts of hops and shorter periods of boiling.

In practice, one to three ounces of hops are boiled for about one hour for flavoring. For finishing, one-half to one ounce of hops is boiled for five to fifteen minutes. The actual amounts and varieties of hops used depend on the type of beer you are brewing, and will be determined from the recipe you are using.

How to Add Hops

Let's assume that you are using a recipe that calls for an unhopped malt extract, and you plan to both flavor and finish with the hopping.

We would dissolve the malt extract in the hot water, as before, and we would bring the mixture back to a boil. At that point we would add the flavoring hops and allow them to boil in the wort for about forty-five minutes.

At the end of this time, we would add the finishing hops to the pot, and continue the boiling for another five to fifteen minutes.

There will be variations in this hopping procedure, depending on the recipe, and whether powdered hops are used.

The total boiling time for complete hopping is about one hour. During this time, the boiling pot should be partially covered with a lid. In this way the wort will retain more of the hop essences, which tend to be driven off with the steam. Again, be careful that the pot doesn't boil over since the lid will retain more of the heat in the pot.

Hops Powder, Pellets

Recently, hops in powdered or pelletized form have become available. These are more concentrated than the dried hops, and some variation in the hopping procedure must be used. For example a 10-gram (⅓-ounce) package of powdered hops is about the same as 1 ounce of regular dried hops.

At left are the dried hops consisting of pieces of the hop blossom. At right, the hops in pelletized form.

Andrea and Fred follow instructions closely when hopping the wort, adding hops exactly as recipe suggests.

Wort is poured through a fine mesh strainer to remove the spent hops. This is done with powdered or pelletized hops.

The boiling time can be reduced somewhat for powdered hops. The flavoring boil can be reduced to thirty minutes, and the finishing to five minutes, when using either powdered or pelletized hops. Also, while it is not entirely necessary to strain out the hops in this form because of the very small particle size, I prefer to strain.

Strain Liquid

The hopping is now completed by pouring the hot liquid through a fine mesh strainer, to remove the spent hops. This straining can be done as you pour the mixture onto the other ingredients in the fermenter. Top up with water as previously described.

If you are using a hopped malt extract but wish to add more hop aroma to the beer, simply do the finishing phase by adding finishing hops for the last five to fifteen minutes of the boil.

Traditionally, hops are obtained in dried form consisting of the whole pieces of the hop blossom. In this form they are often called "leaf hops." The procedure we've just discussed is based on the use of hops in this form.

Variations in Method

You can try several refinements when using the hopping procedure.

One is to divide the flavoring hops into several portions which are added at different points in the boil. For example, the flavoring hops may be divided into two equal portions with one portion added at the beginning of the boil and the other added after twenty to thirty minutes. This gives a good hop flavor but reduces the extraction of bitterness from the hops.

Another variation in the use of finishing hops is to "dry

hop." In dry hopping, the finishing hops are not boiled, but are tied up in a cheesecloth bag and added directly to the fermenter. Dry hopping produces greater hop aroma in the beer without any additional bitterness.

Study the hop table in the section on ingredients before purchasing the hops you use.

Fermentation

Where are we now? We have mixed and boiled the wort, and have hopped it if that was called for in our recipe. Our next step is to ferment this wort.

Fermentation should begin as quickly as possible after we have cooled the wort to 75–80° F. The longer the wort sits, the greater is the chance of "off" ferments taking place because of the action of airborne bacteria. For this reason it is important that the fermenter be kept tightly covered during the cooling process and later.

Preparing the Yeast

Here are two methods for preparing the yeast to be added to the wort. Both of them have the same purposes, to increase the amount of yeast and to get it into its active state.

The first method is to prepare a "starter bottle." Use a sterilized bottle, and a day or two before you will be brewing the beer, make up a small wort by boiling a little malt extract and water and put it in the bottle. Cover the bottle with a piece of plastic secured by a rubber band around the neck of the bottle. When this small wort has cooled to 75–80° F., add the yeast, then mix them by shaking the bottle. Place the plastic wrap over the top again.

Within a few hours the small wort will start to ferment.

Fred raises the plastic to take the temperature of the cooling
wort. It should be between 75° and 80° F.

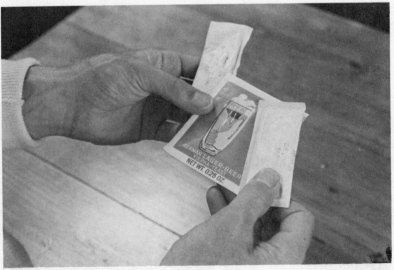

Here are several of the yeasts that can be used in making beer.
Don't use ordinary yeast or baker's yeast.

To prepare yeast, Fred adds it to a small amount of wort in a starter bottle. He shakes it, then covers top with plastic.

Next step: add the yeast to the wort, replace the cover with the fermentation lock. Bubbles should rise within twenty-four hours.

The contents of the starter bottle, which will be about one pint in volume, can then be added to the main wort and stirred in.

Use of this method gets the wort off to a very fast start because the yeast is already in active ferment when it is added.

Second method

Most beer yeasts that are now available will start fermenting rather quickly if activated in warm water before mixing with the wort. For this reason, the second method of preparing the yeast is acceptable. This method involves stirring the yeast in a little water that has been heated to about 100° F. This is mixed into the wort, and fermentation should start within twelve to twenty-four hours.

After mixing the yeast with the wort, secure the lid of the single-stage fermenter, and insert the fermentation lock, with water added, in the lid.

Within about twenty-four hours bubbles should be rising through the fermentation lock, indicating the start of fermentation.

If no bubbles are rising, check to make sure there are no leaks around the lock.

If everything seems to be airtight, the lid should be removed from the fermenter and the wort examined for signs of fermentation. If the wort is fermenting, you will see small patches of foam on the surface or tiny pinpoint bubbles popping to the surface. If the wort is quiet, stir it and wait another twelve hours. If fermentation has not begun then, prepare another yeast starter and add it to the wort.

Vigorous Activity

If you are using the two-stage method, you will see the fermentation activity in the primary fermenter by looking through its plastic cover.

After the start of fermentation there will be vigorous activity for about two days. A layer of foam will cover the surface of the liquid, and the gas will bubble rapidly through the fermentation lock, if you are using the single-stage method. *With the two-stage method, a layer of foam forms within twenty-four hours, and the plastic cover will billow from the escaping gas.*

In both methods, the activity will subside in about two days, with the foam layer diminishing and the rate of bubbling dropping off.

Skim the Foam Layer?

There's a controversy among brewers regarding the foam layer that forms during the first day or two of fermentation. You will notice that it has brownish patches on top of it. This

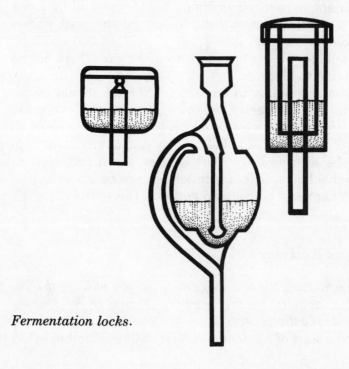

Fermentation locks.

scum is caused by the bitter resins from the hops. Some brewers claim that this scum should be skimmed off to prevent excessive bitterness in the beer. Other brewers disagree.

My experience has been that it makes little difference except possibly when making very light and mild beers. If I am making a very light beer I will skim off the hop scum at some point before the head drops with the end of fermentation. If you wish to do this, remove the lid or cover from the fermenter after the first day of fermentation and skim off the scum with a large spoon. No harm is done by removing the lid or cover at this stage because the large volume of carbon dioxide gas being generated will immediately drive off any air that may enter the fermenter.

Time to Test

In five to seven days after the start of fermentation, the bubbles in the lock of the single-stage fermenter will have slowed to one every few minutes or none at all. When no bubbles are observed in the lock, fermentation is probably complete. At this point, or when you are ready for bottling, remove a small sample from the fermenter and take a hydrometer reading. If the terminal gravity mentioned in the recipe has been reached, it's time for priming and bottling. If the terminal gravity has not been reached, replace the fermenter lid and wait a few more days before testing again.

With the two-stage method, when the foam layer subsides, the beer must be transferred by siphoning into the secondary fermenter and a fermentation lock fitted to the secondary fermenter.

Avoid aerating the beer when siphoning. This is done by running the end of the siphon tube all the way to the bottom of the secondary fermenter to minimize splashing.

Do not siphon from the bottom of the primary fermenter. By avoiding this, you will not transfer sediment to the secondary fermenter.

With two-stage method, siphon beer into secondary fermenter (on floor). Run tube to bottom of fermenter so beer doesn't splash.

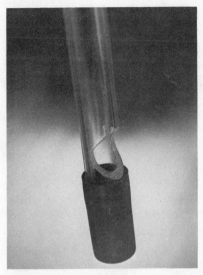 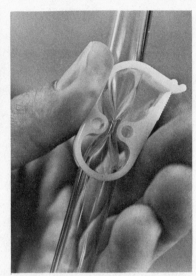

This device (left) prevents you from siphoning sediment. The siphon clamp (right) prevents spills and maintains the suction.

Fermentation lock is shown mounted in the stopper of the five-gallon carboy used as a secondary fermenter.

The fermentation is completed in the secondary fermenter in essentially the same way as in the single-stage fermenter; that is, the absence of bubbles signals that a hydrometer reading should be taken to check for terminal gravity. This usually occurs about five days after transfer to the secondary fermenter.

May Take Longer

The length of time for complete fermentation will be longer if fermentation takes place at temperatures below 70° F. The lower the temperature, the longer fermentation will take. The cooler temperatures generally mean a better quality beer, but don't attempt fermentation below 55–60° F., until you have gained some experience, because fermentation at temperatures that low can be tricky.

About five days after first steps, Fred tests beer with hydrometer to find whether terminal gravity has been reached.

As a practical matter, the possible advantages of fermenting below 55° may not be worth the increased waiting time.

Reading the Hydrometer

If you are in doubt about how to read the hydrometer to decide whether terminal gravity has been reached, reread the material in the section under Equipment.

A few other generalizations about terminal gravity. When you have reached that point with your batch of beer, the beer is ready to be primed and bottled. The beer should be bottled within a few days after the fermentation is reached, but the

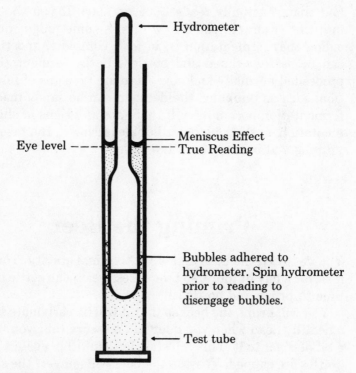

Reading the Hydrometer.

actual time of bottling is not critical so long as the fermentation lock is kept in place. This means, of course, that you can bottle the beer when it's most convenient for you to do so.

It is a good practice to let the beer settle out for a day or two after fermentation ceases. This allows excess yeast to settle out of the beer and, therefore, minimizes the yeast deposit in the bottle. After settling for a day or two, the beer should be fairly bright and clear.

You must do some interpreting with the figures obtained in the final hydrometer reading. A good recipe specifies the expected terminal gravity. Due to normal variations in ingredients you may find the terminal gravity is slightly higher or lower than that indicated in the recipe. For example, the expected terminal gravity may be given as 1.004 but you may find that it actually reads 1.005 or 1.006. If you should run into this situation, you'll have to use some judgment in deciding that fermentation is, in fact, complete, and the beer can be safely primed and bottled. If the fermentation has proceeded normally and now there are no signs of fermentation, such as bubbling, the decision can be safely made that fermentation is complete. If there are any signs of slight fermentation, such as pinpoint bubbles rising in the beer, delay priming and bottling for a few days.

Priming the Beer

You've tested the beer, and it's at terminal gravity. You've let it sit for a day or more, so that excess yeast can settle out. It's time to prime and bottle it.

You will prime the beer so that it will be carbonated—have a healthy head when you pour it. To assure this, you will add a bit of sugar to it. This will start fermentation again after the bottles are capped. Yeast in the beer will convert the sugar to alcohol and carbon dioxide gas. And we want the latter, because that is what will bubble forth when we open the bottles.

Caps and Bottles

By this time you should have checked to make certain your capper is ready, you have enough caps, and the bottle supply is both adequate and clean.

If you've already cleaned the bottles as discussed in the earlier section on sanitation, you need only run them through the hot rinse and dry cycle of the dishwasher—again avoid using soap or detergent. Or you can sterilize them with a sterilizing solution made up of two tablespoons of bleach in two quarts of water. A simple way to use this is to place the solution in a plastic squeeze bottle. Insert the bottle tip into each bottle and squirt in some of the solution. Swirl it around, then let the bottles sit for a few minutes. Rinse with hot water and turn mouth-down to drain and dry. The bottles are ready for filling when they are dry.

Add Sugar

Measure out one level teaspoon of corn sugar into each twelve-ounce bottle, or two teaspoons if you are using champagne bottles. If you like a more effervescent beer, use one and a quarter teaspoons of corn sugar per bottle.

Priming is much easier if the bottles are completely dry. If the bottle necks are wet, the sugar tends to stick to the neck and cause difficulty. As an aid to priming, you can make a funnel from stiff paper, or use a small plastic funnel with all but a short section of the spout cut off.

Fill Bottles

After priming, each bottle is filled to within about 1½ inches from the top, and capped. After you have filled and capped all the bottles, grasp each bottle by the neck and rock it back and forth rapidly. This will mix and dissolve the priming sugar.

It's ready to be bottled. Andrea primes each bottle with sugar to carbonate the drink.

Getting ready to siphon beer into bottles, Andrea fills tube with beer. Note siphon clamp on hose.

Success. The beer begins to flow into the bottle, and the two carefully fill each bottle to 1½ inches from top.

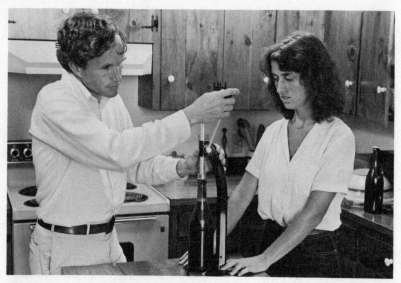

Several models of cappers are available. This bench capper is fastest to use, but is the most expensive.

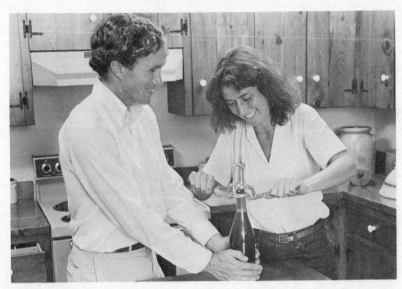

The hand lever capper is less expensive than the bench capper, but Andrea finds it tests her strength.

Cheapest, but more difficult to use effectively, is the hammer capper. Some, like Fred, aren't comfortable with it.

When capped, the bottle should be tipped back and forth, to mix sugar and start the carbonation.

This method should be used for single-stage fermentation and can be used for the two-stage method. Another way to prime, for the two-stage method, is to siphon the beer back from the secondary fermenter to the primary fermenter, then add the sugar in the primary fermenter at a rate of 1 to 1¼ cups per 5 gallons of beer.

If you use this method, make certain the sugar is dissolved and evenly distributed, by stirring thoroughly. I have found that I could accomplish this better if I placed the sugar in the primary fermenter, then siphoned the beer into the fermenter, mixing as it flowed in.

Yet another system of priming can be used with either method. That is to prepare a sugar syrup. Measure out 1½ level cups of corn sugar and add exactly 1 cup of water. Mix in a small saucepan. Stir thoroughly and bring to a simmer. Do not let the mixture boil for more than one minute or too much water will be evaporated away, and this will upset the proportions in the mixture.

After simmering, the volume of the mixture should be twelve fluid ounces. One teaspoon of this liquid will then be equivalent to one teaspoon of dry sugar.

For bulk priming 5 gallons of beer, use 1–1¼ cups of this syrup. Use 1–1¼ teaspoons per 12-ounce bottle.

Priming with the syrup is easier because the syrup can be poured into the bottles. Use a small funnel and bottle priming will go quickly and smoothly.

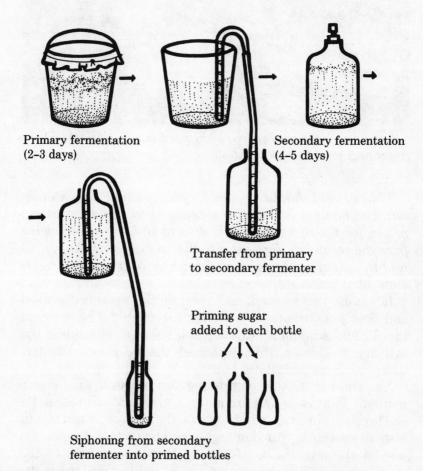

Primary fermentation
(2–3 days)

Secondary fermentation
(4–5 days)

Transfer from primary
to secondary fermenter

Priming sugar
added to each bottle

Siphoning from secondary
fermenter into primed bottles

Two-stage fermentation.

Aging

After bottling and capping, the beer must undergo a small fermentation in the bottle to become carbonated. This takes about two weeks at room temperature during which time the beer will become carbonated and will clear. A small yeast deposit will form on the bottom of the bottle.

During this period the bottles should be standing upright in cartons. Give each bottle a shake two or three days after bottling. This aids bottle fermentation and the clearing process. For best conditioning and overall quality, the beer should be stored at a temperature of 60-70° F. This promotes a slower rate of fermentation than storage at higher temperatures, and means more complete absorption of the gas into the beer. A properly conditioned beer will produce a fine bead (bubbles rising in the beer) and a good head when poured for serving. An improperly conditioned beer will show relatively large bubbles rising rapidly in the glass so that the sparkle and head disappear rather rapidly and the beer quickly becomes flat. A flat beer can indicate storage at too high temperatures, or insufficient priming sugar.

Wait

After the beer has cleared, in about two weeks, you may start drinking it. However, it has not yet reached its full potential of quality. Give it another two to four weeks and there will be a very significant increase in quality. Your wait will be well rewarded.

During this period the beer should be stored in a heavy cardboard carton, and placed in a location where curious children will not have access to it. If you should make a mistake and bottle the beer with too much sugar in it, the bottles could explode. Be on the safe side and store the beer in a safe place.

Serving

It's been a long six weeks, but you've waited. You've cooled a bottle to just the degree of coldness you prefer. You snap off the cap.

Take it easy. Remember, there's a small yeast deposit on the bottom of the bottle. Every naturally carbonated beer has it.

If this yeast deposit is poured with the beer it will do you no harm—it's loaded with beneficial vitamins. However it will cloud up the beer and give it an undesirable yeasty taste.

To avoid this, pour carefully to decant the clear beer off the sediment. This is a very slight inconvenience at first, but after you have poured a few bottles it will become a natural thing to do.

Here's the technique: pour the beer slowly so that it flows smoothly. Hold the bottle so that the light is entering the bottle opposite to you. In that way you can see when the yeast starts to enter the neck of the bottle, and you will cease pouring. With a little practice, you can pour down to within a half-inch of the bottom without a trace of yeast entering your glass.

To minimize the bottle-cleaning job for future batches, develop the habit of rinsing the sediment out of each bottle immediately after pouring the beer.

Draft Beer

Most of us prefer draft beer over canned or bottled beer. The reason is that draft beer has not been pasteurized and therefore retains a fresher, fuller flavor. Since home-brewed beer is not pasteurized, it naturally has the same advantage that commercial draft beer has even though it is bottled.

They've waited six—well four—weeks, and it's time to get out the mugs and see whether it was all worthwhile.

You'll be as proud as they were with their first attempt at making beer. "It's great," they agreed.

But perhaps you would like to have home-brewed draft beer. It's possible, although it adds to the expense.

You can buy a pressurized keg for about $85. This keg usually has a capacity of five or six gallons and is equipped with a carbon dioxide injector that uses small sparklet cartridges as a source of carbon dioxide gas. As the beer is drawn from the spigot, the injector automatically releases gas into the keg to keep the head space pressurized. Of course you must have an extra refrigerator to keep the beer chilled.

My experience with these kegs has been reasonably satisfactory. The big drawback has been that it takes a good many sparklet cartridges to keep the keg pressurized as the beer is dispensed.

I expect that improved draft dispensing systems will soon be available to make this approach more practical and appealing.

If you do decide to keg the beer, remember that it must be primed with sugar in the usual manner when it is placed in the keg.

HOT WEATHER BREWING

If you're like me, you may want more beer during the hot weather season. And that's the time it's more difficult to keep the wort cool enough to produce an excellent beer.

There's a trick that you can use to get around this.

The trick is to place your fermenter in a water bath. To do this, simply place the fermenter in a good-sized tub or plastic trash can with enough cool water in it to cover about the bottom third of the fermenter. Drape old towels over the top of the fermenter and extend them down into the water. The water is soaked up by the towels and is evaporated into the air, thus cooling the brew.

Recipes for Using Malt Extracts

Numerous recipes for home-brewed beer have been published in books and periodicals. The variations in these recipes reflect the differences in individual brewer's tastes as well as each one's particular experience in brewing. Some of these recipes are designed to duplicate particular commercial beers.

Since it's impossible to look at a particular recipe and predict what the resulting beer will taste like, it is practically necessary for the beginning home brewer to try a particular recipe and judge the final result by tasting. You may have to make several batches before you find exactly what you are looking for. Bear in mind that the same recipe made from different brands of malt extract can produce quite different beers.

The suggested approach is first to select a recipe for the general type of beer desired, such as light, amber, or dark. This is further refined by other descriptions given in the recipe, such as American-style light, European-style light, English pale ale type, and Irish stout type. Based on this information, you select a recipe to be tried. With some experience you will be able to modify recipes to suit your particular taste or even design new recipes.

The recipes given in this section are basic ones. They cover the spectrum of beer types and have proven to yield quality beers. I have avoided specifying brand names, but by referring to the table of malt extracts, page 18, you can readily select an appropriate brand of malt extract for each recipe. This table is by no means exhaustive, but these are brands that I have found to give good results. The picture regarding commercial extracts is changing rapidly, with new products being introduced, so that the prospects for a wider selection of quality malts are quite encouraging.

A desired temperature range for fermentation is given in each recipe. This is the temperature range for best results. If you are not able to maintain the specified temperatures, ferment at whatever temperature you can maintain, so long as it's not over 75° F. Fermentation at temperatures above this level is not conducive to the production of quality beers.

Five-Gallon Recipes

All the recipes are for producing five U.S. gallons. If you are accustomed to Imperial measure, the volume would be four Imperial gallons.

Some recipes are based on using hopped malt extracts and some are based on unhopped malt extracts with the addition of hops. In general, the recipes which use hops produce better beers, but perfectly good beers can be made from hopped extracts as well.

Small variations in quantities of ingredients can be tolerated without any really significant effect on the final product. For example, if the recipe calls for 3.3 or 3.5 pounds of malt extract, but you have a 3-pound can, you can either ignore this small difference or, if you desire, you could add an additional cup of corn sugar to make up the difference. On the other hand, this should not imply that you can be sloppy in the use of ingredients, particularly if you are striving for consistent production of a favorite recipe. Your judgment on acceptable variations of ingredients will be sharpened by experience and maintaining a record of what variations are tried.

BASIC BEER

5 U.S. Gallons

3.3-3.5 pounds unhopped malt syrup (light, amber, or dark)
3 cups corn sugar*
2 teaspoons gypsum or Burton water salts
1 teaspoon table salt
⅓-1 ounce (10-30 grams) Hallertauer powdered or pelletized hops
1 package lager beer yeast

This recipe can be used as a basis for a number of different beers by varying the type of malt and the amount of hops used. Refer to the table on malts, page 18, to select an appropriate malt. Use a light malt for a light beer, an amber malt for an amber beer, and dark malt for a dark beer. For a lightly hopped beer, use ⅓ ounce (10 grams) of hops. For a medium hopped beer, use ⅔ ounce (20 grams) of hops. For a highly hopped beer, use 1 ounce (30 grams) of hops. Remember that this recipe calls for powdered or pelletized hops and not dried, or leaf, hops.

Follow instructions in preceding section. Ferment at 55-65° F. If using ⅓ ounce of hops, boil the wort for 25-30 minutes with all of the hops. If using ⅔ ounce of hops, divide hops into three equal parts and boil two parts of the hops for 25 minutes, then add the remaining one part of hops and boil for an additional 5 minutes. If using 1 ounce of hops, divide hops into four equal parts and boil three parts for 25 minutes, then add remaining part of hops and boil for an additional 5 minutes.

After completing boil, pour hot wort through a fine mesh strainer onto corn sugar, gypsum or Burton salts and table salt in the fermenter and mix thoroughly. Top up to 5 gallons volume with water and add yeast starter when temperature has dropped to 75-80° F.

---

* Plus 1-1¼ cups for priming at terminal gravity of 1.004 or below.

This basic beer recipe produces full-flavored, full-bodied beers more in the European or Canadian style. The procedure is simple and straightforward, and you will find that these basic beers are of excellent quality. The selection of malt types and hop quantities will depend on your own personal taste.

You will note that this recipe calls for the use of table salt. Most of the other recipes in the book do not. I have found that the addition of one teaspoon of table salt brings out the full flavor of the beer. You may add one teaspoon of table salt to any of the other recipes in the book as your discretion dictates.

LIGHT BEER, AMERICAN STYLE

5 U.S. Gallons

2.2–2.5 pounds light hopped malt syrup
3 cups (1¼ pounds) corn sugar*
1 teaspoon table salt
1 package lager beer yeast
½ ounce finishing hops (optional)

Follow instructions in preceding section. Ferment at 55–65° F. If finishing hops are used, add for final 10 minutes of boil. Use ½ ounce of Cascade or Hallertauer dried hops or 1/6 ounce (5 grams) of powdered hops.

A good variation of this recipe is to use an unhopped malt and to use the hopping procedure just described for Basic Beer.

* Plus 1–1¼ cups for priming at terminal gravity of 1.002 or below.

LIGHT BEER, EUROPEAN STYLE

5 U.S. Gallons

3.3–3.5 pounds light hopped malt syrup
3 cups (1¼ pounds) corn sugar*
1 package lager beer yeast
2 teaspoons gypsum or Burton water salts (optional)
½ ounce finishing hops (optional)

Proceed as described in preceding section. Ferment at 55–65° F. If finishing hops are used, add for final 10 minutes of boil. Use ½ ounce of Cascade or Hallertauer dried hops or 5 grams of powdered hops. If gypsum or Burton salts are used, stir into hot water just prior to dissolving malt. Use of these water hardeners will intensify the flavor of the beer somewhat.

• If you wish to make this into an all-malt beer, substitute 3 cups of light dried malt extract for the 3 cups of corn sugar. The all-malt version will be more full-bodied and will have more malt flavor. Terminal gravity may be slightly higher than 1.004 but do not bottle until it falls below 1.006.

* Plus 1–1¼ cups for priming of terminal gravity of 1.004 or below.

AMBER ALE, ENGLISH TYPE

5 U.S. Gallons

3.3-3.5 pounds amber hopped malt syrup
4 cups (2 pounds) light dried malt extract
6 teaspoons gypsum or Burton water salts
1 ounce Fuggles flavoring hops
½ ounce Fuggles finishing hops
1 package ale yeast
1-1¼ cups corn sugar for priming

Follow instructions in previous section. Ferment at 65-70°
F. Stir in gypsum or Burton salts just before dissolving malt.
Total boil time is one hour. Boil 1 ounce flavoring hops for
last 30 minutes of boil. Boil ½ ounce of finishing hops for the
final 5 minutes of boil. Ferment down to terminal gravity of
1.007 or below.

DARK BEER, EUROPEAN STYLE

5 U.S. Gallons

3.3-3.5 pounds dark hopped malt syrup
4 cups (1½ pounds) corn sugar*
1 package lager beer yeast
½ ounce finishing hops (optional)

Follow instructions in previous section. Ferment at 55-65°
F. Total boil time may be extended to one hour if desired. If
finishing hops are used, add them for final 10 minutes of boil.
Use ½ ounce of Cascade or Hallertauer dried hops or 1/6
ounce (5 grams) of powdered hops.

* Plus 1-1¼ cups for priming at terminal gravity of 1.004 or below.

• A heavier, more flavorful beer can be made by substituting 4 cups of dried malt extract for the 4 cups of corn sugar. Terminal gravity for this version may be slightly higher than 1.004 but do not bottle until it falls below 1.006.

MEDIUM STOUT

5 U.S. Gallons

6.6–7.0 pounds dark hopped malt syrup
½ ounce finishing hops
1 package ale yeast
1–1¼ cups corn sugar for priming

Follow instructions in previous section. Ferment at 65–70° F. Total boil time should be extended to one hour. Use Cascade or Fuggles hops for finishing. Add finishing hops for final 5 minutes of boil. This brew will take longer to ferment out than others because of the high malt content. Allow to ferment to terminal gravity of 1.015 or below. Do not be in a hurry to bottle this brew; let it ferment down as far as it will go before priming. Stouts also benefit more than lighter beers from longer aging. Age for three months for best results.

LIGHT SUMMER BEER

5 U.S. Gallons

6 cups (3 pounds) light dried malt extract
2 cups (¾ pound) corn sugar*
⅔ ounce (20 grams) powdered Hallertauer hops
2 teaspoons gypsum or Burton water salts
1 package lager beer yeast

Follow instructions in previous section. Ferment at 55–65° F. Stir in gypsum or Burton salts just before dissolving the malt. Divide the hops into three equal parts. Add the first third to the wort and boil for 20 minutes and then add the next third and boil for an additional 20 minutes. At the end of this 40-minute boil period, add the remaining third of the hops and boil for another 5 minutes.

* Plus 1–1¼ cups for priming at terminal gravity of 1.004 or below.

LOW-ALCOHOL LIGHT BEER

5 U.S. Gallons

3.3–3.5 pounds unhopped light malt
2 teaspoons gypsum or Burton water salts
1 teaspoon table salt
⅓–⅔ ounce (10–20 grams) Hallertauer powdered or pelletized hops
1 package lager beer yeast
1–1¼ cups for priming at terminal gravity of 1.004 or below

This is the same recipe as Basic Beer except that the sugar is left out. The result is a beer of slightly more than 3 percent alcohol—a good thirst quencher.

Follow the instructions in the preceding section. Ferment at 55–65° F. For a lightly hopped beer, use ⅓ ounce of hops and boil the wort for 25–30 minutes with all of the hops. For a more highly hopped beer, use ⅔ ounce, divide the hops into three equal parts. Boil two parts of the hops for 25 minutes, then add the remaining part and boil for an additional 5 minutes.

After completing boil, pour hot wort through a fine mesh strainer onto the gypsum or Burton salts and table salt in the fermenter and mix thoroughly. Top up to 5 gallons with water and add yeast starter when temperature has dropped to 75–80° F.

CHAMPAGNE BEER

5. U.S. Gallons

6 cups (3 pounds) light dried malt extract
4 cups (32 ounces) white grape juice
10 grams (⅓ ounce) powdered Hallertauer hops
1 package lager beer yeast
1¼ cups corn sugar for priming

Follow instructions in previous section. Ferment at 55–65° F. Boil hops with malt for 25 minutes. Add white grape juice along with water to make up to 5 gallons. Ferment down to terminal gravity of 1.004 or below. Bulk prime with 1¼ cups of corn sugar or prime each 12-ounce bottle with 1¼ teaspoons.

AMERICAN STEAM BEER

5 U.S Gallons

6 cups (3 pounds) light dried malt extract OR
3.5 pounds unhopped light malt syrup
4 cups (2 pounds) amber dried malt extract OR
2.2 pounds unhopped amber malt syrup
2 ounces Cascade flavoring hops
½ ounce Cascade finishing hops
1 teaspoon gypsum or Burton water salts
1 package lager beer yeast
1-1¼ cups corn sugar for priming

Follow instructions in preceding section. Ferment at 60-70° F. Stir in water hardener just prior to dissolving the malt. Because of the high malt content, the wort should be made up to at least 2 gallons for boiling or split into two batches.

Use Cascade hops for both flavoring and finishing. Divide flavoring hops into two equal parts, add one-half at beginning of boil and boil for 30 minutes. Add other half of flavoring hops and boil for another 15 minutes, then add finishing hops and boil for additional 10 minutes for total boil time of 55 minutes. Ferment down to terminal gravity of 1.007 or below.

Advanced Brewing

The first part of this book deals with the basic procedures for brewing with malt extracts. The essential difference between those basic brewing procedures and the more advanced procedures in this section is that now we will cover the use of grains in brewing. The reason for using grains is that the very finest beers are brewed from grains, either by using grains exclusively, or in combination with malt extracts. The use of grains, principally pale malted barley, also provides a greater range of different types of quality beers that can be made.

All of the procedures discussed earlier apply also to brewing with grains. The use of grains only requires an additional step wherein you produce your own *malt extract* through the process of *mashing*.

Simply stated, mashing involves cooking malted barley in water at certain temperatures to convert the grain starches to fermentable sugars. In cases where relatively large proportions of grains are used, mashing also modifies the protein materials in the grain so that the excess protein can be eliminated from the wort by boiling. If this excess protein material is not eliminated, the beer will not clear properly, or will tend to develop a haze when chilled. When only small proportions

75

of grain are used, protein clarification is not so important and a simplifed mashing procedure can be used.

Contrary to what you may have read elsewhere, mashing is not difficult and does not require elaborate equipment. The only additonal item of equipment you will need is an immersion-type thermometer which covers the range of about 0–220° F.

Ingredients for Advanced Brewing

All of the ingredients listed earlier are also used in the more advanced procedures. These include malt extracts, hops, corn sugar, and yeast. The principal additional ingredient used in advanced brewing is pale malted barley, called simply *pale malt*. Other special malts, such as crystal and black malts, will also be used in small amounts in certain beers. In commercial brewing, particularly in the United States, other grains such as rice and corn are used. These are called *malt adjuncts* and are always used in conjunction with pale malt. Malt adjuncts provide a less expensive source of fermentable sugars, and when substituted for a portion of the malt, will produce lighter beers.

In the following paragraphs we will provide some information relative to the characteristics and use of the primary malts and malt adjuncts. This will assist in understanding the role each plays in a particular recipe and will help in understanding the nature of the mashing process.

Pale Malted Barley (Pale Malt)

Pale malt is produced from raw barley through malting. Malting is a very specialized process that is not normally attempted by the home brewer, but you should understand the principles of malting as an aid to a complete understanding of mashing.

Malting is carried out as follows. The raw barley is steeped in water until it germinates or sprouts. During this germination period two types of enzymes are produced. These are called amylase and proteinase. The amylase enzymes have the power to convert starches to other substances when activated at certain temperatures. The proteinase enzyme has the power to break down protein materials when activated at certain temperatures. Specifically, the amylase enzymes are composed of two components—alpha-amylase and beta-amylase. Alpha-amylase is most active in the temperature range of 150–155° F. and converts starch to maltose sugar and nonfermentable dextrins. Beta-amylase is most active in the temperature range 130–140° F. and primarily converts starch to fermentable maltose sugar. Proteinase is most active at about 115–120° F.

Two types of malt

As the germination of the grain proceeds, the proteinase enzyme converts more and more of the protein materials, but the strength of the amylase enzyme decreases. If the germination process is stopped early, by drying the grain in a kiln, the resulting malt will have high amylase strength but will also have a large amount of unconverted protein. This type of malt is said to be under-modified.

Conversely, if the germination is allowed to proceed further, the resulting malt would be low in amylase strength but would have most of the protein converted. This type of malt is said to be fully modified.

Malts produced in the United States are almost always of the under-modified type while European malts, particularly those made in England, are usually fully modified. This is because most commercial breweries in the United States use malt adjuncts and need the extra amylase strength to convert the starches in these adjuncts. Knowledge of which type malt you are using can be useful in mashing. More attention must

Malts include these three: From left are pale malt, black malt and crystal malt. Roasting time governs color of malt.

be given to protein conversion when under-modified malt is used.

Pale malt thus produced is pale in color and is the primary basis for most beers. Pale malt is approximately 70 percent starch by weight. It will be the principal ingredient to be used in making all-grain beers or beers made from a combination of malt extract and grain.

Crystal Malt

Crystal malt, sometimes called caramel malt, is amber in color and somewhat sweeter than pale malt. It has been processed so that most of the starch is already converted to sugar, but the grain is lightly roasted so that the sugar has been caramelized. A small amount of fermentable sugar remains in the grain after roasting.

Crystal malt is used in small amounts to add color and flavor to ales and dark beers. Usually it is not necessary to mash crystal malt since it has very little starch content and is used in small amounts. It is usually added at some point to the wort boil to extract its color and flavor, although it can be mashed with the pale malt if pale malt is also used in the recipe.

Black Malt

Black malt is, as you might expect, black or dark brown in color. It is a heavily roasted malt which provides intense color and flavor to the brew. It is used in small amounts in recipes for dark beers and stouts. Black malt contains no fermentable sugars so that all the solids extracted from it remain in the finished beer. Because of its strong flavor, it is usually cooked whole, without crushing, except in brewing stouts where a half-pound or so may be crushed.

Corn

Corn is one of the principal malt adjuncts. It is used primarily as a source of starch in the mash and does not add any particular character to the beer. It may be used in home brewing in the form of corn grits, cornmeal, or other readily available forms. Corn, as well as other malt adjuncts, should be cooked to a gelatinized form before you add it. This results in more efficient starch conversion during mashing. No more than one part corn, or other malt adjunct, per two parts of pale malt should be used, otherwise complete starch conversion may not take place due to insufficient enzymes.

Rice

Rice plays a role similar to corn in brewing. It is said to provide a certain crispness to light beers. One commercial brewer of a very popular light American beer states on the label that rice is used in its brew. The best rice for brewing is the brown, unpolished type.

Wheat

Wheat, used in small amounts, is said to improve the quality of the head. A few commercial beers are brewed with wheat. The most notable of these are the German "weiss" beers.

The Mashing Process

As previously mentioned, mashing is the process of cooking malted barley in water to convert the grain starches to fermentable sugars and non-fermentable dextrins and, in some cases, to modify the protein in the malt. These conversions are brought about by the amylase and proteinase enzymes. In order to make these conversions, the mash must be held at the correct temperatures for a sufficient length of time to activate the enzymes and allow them to complete the conversions.

Commercial brewers use two methods of mashing. These are called infusion mashing and decoction mashing. There are many variations within each method depending on the ingredients used and the purposes of the brewer. In home brewing we do not need to be concerned with these complications of the commercial breweries who are dealing with very large volumes. The mashing process that we will use involves four simple steps. These are water treatment, grinding the malt, cooking the malt, and sparging.

Water Treatment

Water treatment involves the addition of water hardeners to the brewing water. The effect of these water hardeners, for purposes of mashing, is to decrease the pH of the mash solution. pH is a measure of the acidity of the solution. The lower the pH, the higher the acidity. The pH scale of measurement goes from 0.0 to 14.0 with a pH of 7.0 indicating a neutral solution; that is, a solution which is neither acidic nor alkaline. Most water supplies have a pH of approximately 7.0, or close to neutral. It has been found from experience that most efficient mashing occurs at a pH of about 5.0. It is important then for efficient mashing that we treat the brewing water to reduce the pH of the mash to a value close to 5.0, which is slightly acidic. This is done by adding water hardeners such as gypsum or Burton salts which react with the malt to produce the desired pH value. An alternate method is to add citric acid to the water, but the use of water hardeners is a better method in most cases.

The addition of hardeners to the water not only affects the efficiency of mashing, but also affects the character of the finished beer. As mentioned earlier, harder water tends to intensify the flavor of the beer. If we desire a mild flavored, light beer of the pilsner type, for example, it would be better to use the acid treatment instead of water hardeners. If you wish to use the acid water treatment use one to two teaspoons of citric acid per five-gallon recipe proportioning the amount of acid used in the mash to the amount of mash water. Some experimentation may be required to settle on the optimum amount of acid for a given recipe.

Water hardness varies depending on where the water comes from. Public water supplies in most areas of the United States are relatively soft—usually from 50 to 150 parts per million total hardness. It is of interest to note that beers are brewed throughout the world from water which is very soft (light pilsners) to very hard (English pale ales), the latter being brewed from water which approaches 2,000 parts per million total hardness.

It is easy to experiment with adjusting your brewing water to specific levels of hardness for particular beer types. Obtain an analysis of your water supply from the local water company. This will indicate the total hardness of the water expressed in parts per million (ppm) or milligrams per liter. Your water may be increased in hardness by adding gypsum or Burton salts. A teaspoon of gypsum or Burton salts added to five gallons will increase the hardness by about 150 ppm.

As an example, suppose you wish to adjust your brewing water to a hardness of 450 ppm. Checking with the water company indicates a natural hardness of 75 ppm. so that the hardness must be increased by 450 minus 75 or 375 ppm. This can be accomplished by adding 2½ teaspoons of gypsum or Burton salts per 5 gallons.

Grinding the Malt

In order to bring the starches, enzymes, and other constituents of the malt into solution in the mash water, the malt must be ground into a coarse "mealy" texture. This is a very important step in the mashing procedure because if the malt is not broken into sufficiently fine particles, some of the starches will not be exposed to the enzymes and will not be utilized to produce the desired extract. On the other hand, if the malt is ground too finely, it will be difficult to strain out when the mash is complete.

A good method of grinding the malt is to place small amounts at a time in a kitchen blender or food processor which is rapidly turned on and off until the desired texture is obtained. When properly ground, every individual grain of the malt will be broken up.

Andrea uses blender to grind malt. Each piece must be broken by blender, but ground malt should be mealy, not as fine as flour.

Fred adds ground malt to heated water, in proportions described in each recipe. Temperatures are not critical.

Cooking the Malt

The malt is cooked in the boiling pot. The mash water is placed in the pot and heated to the desired temperature and the ground malt is stirred in. The amount of water required depends on the amount of malt to be mashed. Too much water tends to dilute the enzymes and too little water may lead to scorching or "hot spots." For mashing one or two pounds of malt, use about a gallon of water. For mashing five or six pounds of malt, use about two gallons of water. (See table.)

The cooking time for mashing will vary from about one hour up to two hours. The one-hour cooking time is for mashing one or two pounds of malt when a combination of malt and malt extract is being used in the recipe. This type of mashing is referred to as *simple mashing* and will be covered in more detail in the section on simple mashing procedure. The two-hour cooking time is required when more than two pounds of malt are being mashed and is accomplished as described in the section on *advanced mashing procedure.*

The mashing temperatures are not very critical. Referring briefly to the accompanying mashing diagram you will see, in fact, that the temperatures are actually ten-degree bands. The general procedure is to heat the mash up to the higher temperature in the band and let it cool to the lower temperature in the band. When it is cooled to the lower temperature, it is heated again to the higher temperature and the cycle is repeated. During this heating and cooling cycle, the mash is stirred occasionally to eliminate "hot spots" and maintain even distribution of the enzymes. This temperature cycling is maintained for the indicated time period or until an iodine starch test indicates that all the starch has been converted.

Iodine starch test

The iodine starch test is a very simple procedure. Remove several tablespoons of liquid from the mash pot after stirring

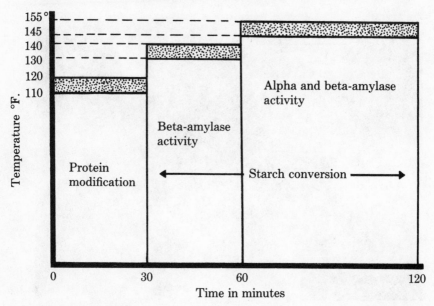

Mashing diagram.

the mixture. Place the liquid in a white saucer. Drop a few drops of tincture of iodine in the saucer. If the liquid turns bluish-purple in color, starch is still present and the mash must continue. If the bluish-purple color does not appear, this indicates that all the starch has been converted and the mash cooking step is complete. Obviously, this test sample should not be added back to the mash as the iodine is toxic.

Sparging

Sparging is the final step in the mashing process. When the mash cooking step is completed, the mash liquid is poured from the boiling pot through a fine mesh strainer into the empty fermenter. The spent malt particles are thus collected and set aside temporarily. Since these spent malt particles still contain a considerable amount of the desired "extract," it

Fred and Andrea pour mash liquid through fine mesh strainer into the empty fermenter to collect spent mash.

is necessary to rinse them with hot water to recover as much as possible of the extract. This rinsing process is called *sparging.*

The term sparging is said to derive from the practice of ancient priests who used green asparagus tips to sprinkle holy water. Sparging water may not have religious significance but it is very important in securing extract from the grain.

To sparge, place the spent malt back in the boiling pot and spray or pour hot water over it and stir. This sparge water, containing the recovered extract, is poured through the strainer into the fermenter and thereby added to the mash liquid. Spent malt may be sparged several times if necessary to recover the desired extract. Care must be taken in sparging, however, not to collect more liquid than can be handled in the boiling pot as all the liquid collected must be boiled to clarify and hop the beer.

Simple Mashing Procedure

If you are mashing no more than two pounds of pale malt, a simpler and shorter mashing procedure may be used. This procedure will use only the final sixty minutes of the mashing cycle shown in the mashing diagram. Specifically, the procedure is as follows.

Place about one gallon of water in the boiling pot and heat to a temperature of 155° F. Stir in the required water treatments as indicated in the recipe. Then stir in the ground malt.

Stirring will cool the mixture slightly so that the temperature should be rechecked after the malt is stirred in. The temperature at this point should be 150–155° F. Allow the mash to cool, stirring occasionally. When it has cooled down to about 145°, heat it up again to 155°. Repeat this cycle as necessary until the sixty-minute mash period is over or the iodine starch test indicates no starch present. Care should be taken in reheating the mash mixture that the temperature does not exceed 160° F. as this may deactivate the enzymes. When the mash cooking step is completed, sparge the spent grains and proceed as indicated in the recipe.

Advanced Mashing Procedure

This procedure must be used when more than two pounds of pale malt are being mashed. For most recipes, this would range from three to seven pounds of malt. To carry out this procedure efficiently your boiling pot should have a capacity of at least five gallons. The advanced mashing procedure encompasses the complete mash cycle as shown in the mashing diagram.

Place the correct amount of water, depending on the

RECOMMENDED VOLUME OF MASH WATER
FOR DIFFERENT AMOUNTS OF GRAIN

Quantity of Grain (lb)	Amount of Mash Water (gal)
3 lb	1½ gal
4	1½
5	2
6	2
7	2½
8	2½

amount of malt to be mashed, in the boiling pot and heat to a temperature of 120° F. Stir in the water treatment and the ground malt. Maintain the mash temperature between 110 and 120° for thirty minutes. This part of the mash cycle serves to modify the protein in the malt.

At the end of this period heat the mash to 140° F. and maintain it between 130° and 140° for an additional thirty minutes. During this period, the beta-amylase enzyme is most active and converts the starch to maltose sugar.

At this point, heat the mixture to 155° F. and maintain the temperature between 145° and 155° for sixty minutes. Often-times this step in the mash cycle can be shortened to thirty to forty-five minutes. For this reason it's a good idea to make an iodine starch test after thirty minutes to see whether all the starch has been converted. This final step in the mash cycle serves to convert starch to non-fermentable dextrins through the action of the alpha-amylase enzyme. Some additional maltose sugar is also produced during this step.

After the mash cooking period is completed, proceed with sparging and preparing the wort as indicated in the recipe.

Having mastered the mashing procedure, you are well on your way to making your finest beers. Mashing involves a little extra effort but you'll find it's worth it when you taste the brew. I usually find it appropriate to enjoy a couple of "cool ones" while the mash is under way as a little reward for the extra effort.

Variations in Mash Cycle

The mashing cycle just described is a good general one and is appropriate for most beer types. This mashing procedure produces an extract which has a relatively high percentage of fermentable maltose sugar and a relatively small percentage of non-fermentable dextrins.

The relative percentages of these two types of extracts can be varied somewhat by changing the mash cycle. For example, if a higher percentage of dextrins is desired for producing heavier beers, this can be done by shortening the time that the mash is held at the 130–140° temperature so that the total beta-amylase activity is reduced, thereby reducing the fermentable sugar extract.

In the extreme case, the 130–140° temperature could be skipped entirely with the entire starch conversion taking place at 145–155° temperature. If this procedure is used, the mash conditions would favor alpha-amylase activity with the development of a higher percentage of dextrins in the extract. This extreme should be approached with caution, however, because it could result in a wort that is out of balance with respect to fermentable sugar and dextrin content. The resulting beer may be too low in alcohol and too "syrupy." Probably, more sensible variation for a heavier beer would be to shorten the 130–140° mash time to, say, fifteen minutes instead of the thirty minutes shown in the mashing diagram.

If you know that you are using fully modified English malt, it is also possible to eliminate the 110–120° protein modification part of the cycle. Here again, caution is advised, however, because you may end up with excessive protein left in the beer. This can lead to problems of clarity in the beer, particularly from hazes developing when the beer is chilled.

These possible variations in the basic mash cycle are a matter of experimentation. If you are venturesome, you may discover some advantages in variations for particular beer.

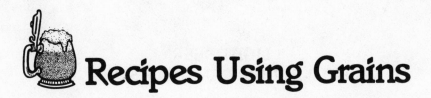 # Recipes Using Grains

The recipes in this section use either a combination of malt extracts and grain, or grain alone. The number of different beers that can be brewed using these types of ingredients is almost endless. With the information in the section on designing recipes, and a little imagination, you can experiment with modifications to the recipes, or try your own. In each recipe, add yeast as explained in Brewing Processes.

LIGHT BEER, ALL GRAIN

5 U.S. Gallons

6 pounds pale malt
2½ ounces dried or 20 grams powdered Hallertauer hops
2 teaspoons gypsum or Burton salts
1-1¼ cups corn sugar for priming*
1 package lager beer yeast

Mash pale malt in 2–2½ gallons of water with 1 teaspoon of water treatment using advanced mashing procedure. Collect

* Prime at terminal gravity of 1.005 or below.

mash and sparge liquid in boiling pot and boil with additional 1 teaspoon of water treatment and hops. Split hops into three equal parts. Add first portion and boil for 30 minutes. Add second portion of hops and boil for additional 20 minutes. Add final portion of hops and boil for 10 minutes. Ferment at 55–65° F.

LIGHT BEER, FULL-BODIED CANADIAN STYLE

5 U.S. Gallons

One day I was sitting on my front porch having a bottle of Molson's lager from Canada when my next-door neighbor showed up with a bottle and two glasses—"Want to try my latest brew?" I was obviously anxious to try it as I had suggested the recipe to him. We proceeded to conduct a side-by-side tasting of his beer with the Molson's. To our surprise the two beers tasted almost identical. Thus, I suggest the following recipe.

3.3–3.5 pounds light unhopped malt syrup
2 pounds pale malt
2 cups (¾ pound) corn sugar*
1 teaspoon gypsum or Burton salts
2½ ounces Cascade or Hallertauer dried hops
1 package lager beer yeast

Mash pale malt using simple mashing procedure with ¼ teaspoon of water treatment. Boil mash liquid and malt extract with 2 ounces of hops for 40 minutes. Add remaining ½ ounce hops and remaining ¾ teaspoon water treatment and boil for additional 10–15 minutes. Strain onto corn sugar in fermenter. Ferment at 55–65° F.

* Plus 1–1¼ cups for priming at terminal gravity of 1.006 or below.

ALL GRAIN, AMERICAN-STYLE
LIGHT BEER

5 U.S. Gallons

This recipe illustrates the use of a malt adjunct, rice in this case, which is very common in commercial brewing in this country. The resulting beer is lightly hopped, light in color and body, and has a light, crisp taste.

4 pounds pale malt
2 pounds whole grain brown rice
2 ounces dried or 20 grams powdered Hallertauer hops
1 teaspoon gypsum or Burton salts
1-1¼ cups corn sugar for priming*
1 package lager beer yeast

Grind rice and boil in water until the rice is soft and gelatinized. Mash pale malt and cooked rice in 1½–2 gallons of water, including the water that the rice was cooked in, and the water treatment. Use advanced mashing procedure. Strain and sparge. Divide hops into 5 equal parts. Boil 2 parts of the hops for 30 minutes. Add another 2 parts of the hops and boil additional 15 minutes. Add last part of hops and boil for additional 5–10 minutes. Ferment at 55–65° F.

* Prime at terminal gravity of 1.004 or below.

AMERICAN STEAM BEER, ALL GRAIN

5 U.S. Gallons

6 pounds pale malt
½ pound crystal malt, cracked
½ pound crystal malt, whole
2½ ounces Cascade dried hops
1 teaspoon gypsum or Burton salts
1-1¼ cups corn sugar for priming*
1 package lager beer yeast

Mash pale malt and cracked crystal malt with 1 teaspoon gypsum or Burton salts in 2-2½ gallons of water using advanced mashing procedure. Boil 2 ounces hops for 45 minutes. Add additional ½ ounce hops, whole crystal malt, and remainder of Burton salts and boil for additional 10 minutes. Ferment at 65-70° F.

* Prime at terminal gravity of 1.007 or below.

LIGHT BEER, GERMAN STYLE

5 U.S. Gallons

2.2-2.5 pounds light unhopped malt syrup
2 pounds pale malt
3 cups corn sugar*
20 grams (⅔ ounce) powdered Hallertauer hops
1 teaspoon gypsum or Burton salts
1 package lager beer yeast

Mash pale malt using simple mashing procedure. Use a quarter of the gypsum or Burton salts in the mash water. Di-

* Plus 1-1¼ cups for priming at terminal gravity of 1.004 or below.

vide hops into five equal parts. Boil mash liquid with remainder of water treatment and four parts of hops for 30 minutes. Add remaining one part of hops and boil for additional 10 or 15 minutes. Pour wort through strainer onto malt syrup and corn sugar in fermenter. Ferment at 55–65° F.

PALE ALE, ENGLISH TYPE

5 U.S. Gallons

2 pounds pale malt
½ pound crystal malt, cracked
½ pound crystal malt, whole
3 pounds light dried malt extract OR
3.5 pounds light unhopped malt syrup
3 ounces Fuggles dried hops
6 teaspoons Burton salts
1–1¼ cups corn sugar for priming*
1 package ale yeast

Mash pale malt and cracked crystal malt with 1 teaspoon Burton salts in one gallon of water, using simple mashing procedure. Boil 2½ ounces hops for 45 minutes. Add additional ½ ounce hops, whole crystal malt, and remainder of Burton salts and boil for additional 10 minutes. Strain onto malt extract in fermenter and ferment at 65–70° F.

* Prime at terminal gravity of 1.008 or below.

STOUT, IRISH TYPE

5. U.S. Gallons

6 pounds dark dried malt extract OR
7 pounds dark unhopped malt syrup
1 pound crystal malt, cracked
½ pound black malt, cracked
3½ ounces Fuggles hops
1-1¼ cups corn sugar for priming*
1 package ale yeast

Dissolve malt extract in at least 2 gallons of water and bring to a boil. Add crystal malt, black malt, and 3 ounces of hops and boil for 55 minutes. Add remaining ½ ounce of hops and boil for additional 5–10 minutes. Strain into fermenter and sparge spent grain. Top up to 5 gallons. Ferment at 65–70° F.

* Terminal gravity of this recipe may be as high as 1.020. Some judgment must be exercised in interpreting the hydrometer reading to determine bottling point as the terminal gravity will vary from batch to batch due to variations in extract from the grains. Keep this brew in fermenter for at least 10 days to make sure it has completely fermented out before priming.

SUPER STOUT

5 U.S. Gallons

This recipe produces a robust, full-bodied stout that compares favorably to Guinness and other similar commercial brews. It has a very high terminal gravity resulting from the roasted grain.

6.6–7.0 pounds dark unhopped malt syrup
½ pound black malt, lightly crushed
2 pounds roasted barley (unmalted) OR
roasted pale malt, lightly crushed
1⅔ ounces (50 grams) pelletized Hallertauer hops
1–1¼ cups corn sugar for priming*
1 package beer yeast

If you cannot obtain roasted barley (unmalted) you may use pale malt and roast it yourself. This is a little more time-consuming, but I have found that it gives excellent results. The procedure for roasting the pale malt is as follows: spread grain, one pound at a time, on a shallow baking pan and roast in a 400° F. oven. Stir the grain frequently for even roasting. Continue roast until all the grains take on a rich brown color.

Dissolve the dark malt syrup in about 2 gallons of water and stir in the crushed black malt and roasted barley or pale malt. Note that the grain is to be lightly crushed, not ground. Bring this mixture to a boil and add 1⅓ ounces (40 grams) of the powdered hops. Boil for 50 minutes. Add the remaining ⅓ ounce (10 grams) of hops and boil for additional 10 minutes. Strain through fine mesh strainer into fermenter and thoroughly sparge the spent grains. Refer to sparging procedure in previous section. Add the sparge liquid to the fermenter and top up with tap water to 5 gallon volume. Ferment at 65–75° F. Age at least three months for best quality.

* Terminal gravity will probably be 1.030 or higher. Leave in fermenter at least 10 days to make sure fermentation is complete before priming and bottling.

DARK BEER, EUROPEAN TYPE

5 U.S. Gallons

4 pounds light dried malt extract OR
5 pounds light unhopped malt syrup
½ pound crystal malt, cracked
½ pound black malt, whole
2 ounces dried or 20 grams powdered Hallertauer hops
1-1¼ cups corn sugar for priming*
1 package lager beer yeast

Dissolve malt extract in at least 2 gallons of water and bring to a boil. Divide hops into three equal parts. Add two portions of hops and crystal malt and boil for 45 minutes. Add black malt, and last portion of hops and boil for 15 minutes. Strain into fermenter and top up to 5 gallons. Ferment at 55–65° F.

* Prime at terminal gravity of 1.007 or below.

LIGHT SUMMER BEER, AMERICAN STYLE

5 U.S. Gallons

3 pounds pale malt
2 cups (1 pound) light dried malt extract
2 cups (¾ pound) corn sugar*
10 grams (⅓ ounce) powdered Hallertauer hops
2 teaspoons gypsum or Burton salts
1 package lager beer yeast

Mash pale malt in 1½–2 gallons of water with 1 teaspoon gypsum or Burton salts, using advanced mashing procedure. Split hops into three equal parts. Boil mash liquid with first portion of hops for 30 minutes; add second portion and boil for additional 20 minutes; add final portion and boil for additional 10 minutes. Strain onto dried malt extract, corn sugar, and one teaspoon gypsum or Burton salts in fermenter. Ferment at 55–65° F.

* Plus 1–1¼ cups for priming at terminal gravity of 1.003 or below.

MAKING TRUE LAGER BEERS

Lager beers are of German origin. True lager beers are made at temperatures of 50° F. or below, and are aged, or lagered, for as much as six months at near-freezing temperatures. The fermentation and aging of the beer at these reduced temperatures impart an added degree of crispness and smoothness to the beer which is not found at higher temperatures. Lager beers are also always fermented from bottom-fermenting, or lager, yeasts.

If you wish to try your hand at producing a true lager, you must have the facilities for maintaining fermentation temperatures down to around 50° F. or below. You can do this very nicely with an extra refrigerator. Try to pick one up second-hand. The refrigerator must be large enough to hold the single-stage or secondary fermenter.

Select a recipe which is appropriate for a lager-type beer, either light or dark. Any of the recipes with recommended fermentation temperature of 55–65° are lager types. Proceed with the fermentation as you would normally. If you are using the single-stage method, allow the wort to come into vigorous fermentation and then place the fermenter in the refrigerator which has been adjusted to a temperature of about 45–50° F. *With the two-stage method, the fermenting wort is placed in the refrigerator after transfer to the secondary fermenter.*

The fermentation will slow down drastically as the temperature of the wort decreases. It may take six to eight weeks for the fermentation to proceed to the bottling point at the reduced temperature. At the end of the fermentation the beer will have cleared and will contain very little live yeast. For this reason it is necessary to make up a yeast starter bottle (see page 44) which is added to the priming sugar at bottling time. This insures that sufficient active yeast is present to ferment out the priming sugar.

Somewhat the same effect can be gained by lagering beer after it is bottled. This procedure is not as good as the one just described but it does improve the quality. To lager in the bottle, you ferment and bottle the beer at normal temperatures and allow the beer to remain at room temperature for two weeks after bottling. This two-week period allows for the complete fermentation of the priming sugar. After the two-week period the beer is stored in the refrigerator at around 40° F. for four or six weeks for the completion of aging.

Designing Your Own Recipes

Part of the fun of advanced brewing is developing your own recipes. You may want to try to duplicate a commercial beer or just create your own unique brew.

To do this systematically, you will need some information regarding the characteristics of the brewing ingredients you are using. Some of this information can only be obtained through experience in using various ingredients but there are certain "constants" that are useful in developing recipes. The most important of these is the percentages of soluble solids (fermentable and non-fermentable) normally found in the various ingredients. The fermentable solids (sugars) determine the alcoholic content of the beer and the non-fermentable solids (primarily dextrins and proteins) make up the body of the beer and determine the terminal gravity. The following table provides some typical values for these percentages. While there are variations in the values, the values given are sufficiently accurate for use in formulating recipes.

By using these constants we would like to be able to predict the percentage of alcohol and the terminal gravity of the finished beer. Unfortunately, this cannot be done with great accuracy. The crux of the problem is that terminal gravity cannot be predicted accurately due to the variations in ingredients. Since we need to know the terminal gravity

TYPICAL PERCENTAGES BY GROSS WEIGHT
OF SOLIDS IN BREWING INGREDIENTS

Ingredient	Percent Fermentable Solids	Percent Non-Fermentable Solids	Percent Total Soluble Solids
Corn sugar	100	0	100
Dried malt extract	80–90	10–20	100
Malt extract syrup	64–72	8–16	80*
Pale malt**	—70 percent starch—		70
Crystal malt	20	50	70
Black malt	0	70	70

* Malt syrups have 20 percent water content.
** Actual percentage of fermentables and non-fermentables depends on particular mashing procedure. Soluble solids also include about 10 percent protein in addition to starch. Protein is ignored in the recipe since it is assumed it is eliminated in the wort by mashing and boiling.

rather accurately for priming and bottling it is necessary to determine this for a new recipe somewhat by trial and error.

It is not necessary to predict the percentage of alcohol with such accuracy. The following formula is usually sufficiently accurate for predicting the percent of alcohol:

The percentage of alcohol by volume equals the starting specific gravity minus 1.000 multiplied by 96.

Here's how to use that rule: for example, a starting specific gravity of 1.040 yields a beer of about 3.8 percent alcohol, computed as follows: 1.040 minus 1.000 times 96 equals 0.040 times 96 or 3.8.

The starting specific gravity can be estimated by virtue of the fact that one pound of solids dissolved in one gallon of water yields a specific gravity of 1.042. For example, if a recipe for five gallons of beer contains a total of four pounds of soluble solids (fermentable and non-fermentable), this is equivalent to 4/5 or 0.8 pounds per gallon. Logically, the starting gravity of this recipe then would be proportionally only 80 percent of one which contained one pound of solids per gallon. The following tabulation can thus be developed which shows the estimated starting gravity and the percent alcohol for different values of solids per gallon.

STARTING SPECIFIC GRAVITY

Solids/Gallon	Starting Gravity	Percent Alcohol
0.7 pounds	1.029	2.7
0.8	1.034	3.3
0.9	1.038	3.7
1.0	1.042	4.0
1.1	1.046	4.4
1.2	1.050	4.8

These calculations are sufficiently accurate for recipes that are based largely on light malts. If more than one pound of crystal or black malts is used, there could be a significant error in the alcohol percentages due to the higher percentage of non-fermentables.

To conclude the discussion on designing recipes, let us analyze a hypothetical recipe to determine solids per gallon, starting gravity, and percent alcohol. The information contained in the table on solids is used here.

HYPOTHETICAL RECIPE FOR 5 U.S. GAL.

Ingredient	Gross Weight of Ingredient	Soluble Solids
Pale malt	2.0 lb	1.4 lb
Light dried malt extract	1.0 lb	1.0 lb
Light malt syrup	2.2 lb	1.8 lb
Crystal malt	0.5 lb	0.4 lb
Corn sugar (priming)	0.4 lb	0.4 lb
	Total	5.0 lb

Soluble Solids/Gal. equals 5 lb. divided by 5 Gal. or 1 lb./Gal.
Starting Gravity: 1.042
Percent Alcohol: 4

A Brief History
Of Home Brewing

Beer has evolved over a period of at least 5,000 years. We don't know how the first brew was made, but we expect it was by accident. One theory is that some prehistoric man set aside some partially chewed grain in a container. He returned to it in a few days to discover, when tasting it, that the fermented grain somehow lifted his spirits.

This theory seems feasible since the enzymes in his saliva could have converted the grain starch to sugar, and wild yeasts could have converted the sugar to alcohol.

The brewing art gradually advanced from this rather unappetizing beginning to more intentional, but still primitive, efforts by early civilized man.

Early writings indicate that at least as far back as 1000 B.C. consumption of fermented grain beverages was commonplace even to the point that they were incorporated into certain religious services in India. The old records found in the valleys of the Euphrates and the Nile deal with raising grain for brewing, and tell recipes for beer-making. Tools of the trade are depicted.

Hops weren't introduced into brewing until about the ninth century, in Germany. Their use became more widespread in the fifteenth century, in England. At that time unhopped beers were called ales. The introduction of hops created a non-alcoholic ferment as the ale brewers looked down upon the use of this "weed."

This original differentiation between ales and beers has lost its meaning because hops are now used in both ales as well as other beers.

Brewing in America

In the American colonies in the seventeenth century beer was the universal beverage that was brewed by practically every pioneer housewife in the home. The universality of the beverage in the early colonies was not only a matter of taste but of health as well. There are many references in the writings of the early settlers to the necessity of drinking beer instead of water to maintain good health. This was probably more of a criticism of the bad drinking water supplies than the quality of the beers of the period. Sir Francis Wyatt, governor of the Virginia colony, wrote to England in 1623 complaining of great sickness in the colony due to a lack of sufficient supplies of beer:

> To plant a colony by water drinkers was an inexcusable errour in these, who layd the first foundacion, and have made it a recieved custome, which until it be laide downe againe, there is small hope of health.*

The early colonial home brewers experienced problems in obtaining adequate supplies of grains, particularly malted barley, and hops to satisfy their brewing needs. Attempts were made to bring in malt and hops from England but this met with limited success. These early settlers had not yet established their crops of barley so they turned to the use of Indian corn, or maize, for their brews. Some use of wild hops is reported but the supply did not meet the demand. Because

---

* Baron, *Brewed in America,* p. 6.

of these shortages of traditional brewing materials, many brewers were forced to make do with substitute ingredients. Brews were concocted from such ingredients as molasses, persimmons, and pumpkins which were flavored with spruce and a variety of other herbs.

A notable example of the use of substitute ingredients, molasses in this case, is found in the following recipe from Colonel George Washington's notebook from the year 1737:

To Make a Small Beer*

Take a large sifter full of Bran Hops to your taste—Boil these 3 hours then strain out 30 gallons into a cooler put in 3 gallons molasses while the beer is scolding hot or rather draw the molasses into the cooler and strain the beer on it while boiling hot. Let this stand till it is little more than blood warm then put in a quart of yeast if the weather is very cold cover it over with a blanket and let it work in the cooler 24 hours then put it into the cask—leave the bung open till it is almost done working—bottle it that day week it was brewed.**

While these drinks made from these non-grain ingredients were not true beers, they nevertheless could be quite palatable. While growing up in South Carolina, I tasted a persimmon beer which was brewed by an uncle each fall. This beer had a pleasingly sharp, zesty flavor with a hint of sweetness and a slight sparkle. Presumably, the basic recipe and procedure which my uncle used originated in the colonies and was passed along from generation to generation. The procedure went approximately as follows.

The persimmon beer was brewed in a large oak barrel which was turned on end with a spigot inserted near the bottom. The barrel was placed in a shed where it was exposed to outside temperatures. The brew was started in the late fall after the first frost. The ingredients consisted of ripe persimmons, ripe "beans" from the locust tree, water, sugar, and

---

* "Small Beer" was a weak beer which was intended to be drunk immediately.
** Washington's Recipe courtesy of New York Public Library.

molasses (in what proportions I do not know). Then persimmons and locust beans were placed in the barrel in alternate layers separated by a layer of clean straw. The barrel was then filled with a mixture of water, sugar, and molasses, and the open end of the barrel was covered. The fermentation proceeded slowly due to the seasonally cool temperatures. When the beer was judged to be ready, it was drawn off from the spigot, the layers of straw serving as a filter of sorts.

Thomas Jefferson could readily be titled the "gentleman brewer" of the early part of the nineteenth century.*

An entry in Jefferson's farm journal dated September 13, 1813, indicates the beginning of his home brewing experience when he wrote "we are this day beginning under the direction of Captain Miller, the business of brewing malt liquers." Captain Joseph Miller was a sea captain who had previously worked in a brewery in England and had thereby gained a knowledge of the "art and mystery" of brewing. Miller was a guest at Monticello for a considerable period of time while Jefferson assisted him in resolving some legal problems. During his stay Miller instructed Jefferson and one of his servants, Peter Hemings, in malting grain and brewing beer.

One indication of Jefferson's serious interest in the subject was that he had in his library at least three books on brewing. Apparently, his favorite book was one written by an English brewer, Michael Combrune, whose book, "The Theory and Practice of Brewing," was published in 1762. By virtue of information gained from his books, and in large measure the instruction by Captain Miller, Jefferson and Peter Hemings became proficient in brewing, primarily with corn and wheat, as barley was not grown at Monticello. This knowledge was spread to other plantations in the area by Jefferson's willingness to make Peter Hemings available to assist in the brewing activities of his neighbors as well as lending them his brewing

---

* I am indebted to Mr. James A. Bear Jr., curator of Monticello, for his assistance in researching Jefferson's brewing activities.

books. Jefferson's brewing activities continued right up to his death on July 4, 1826.

Around the mid-point of the nineteenth century, very significant changes in American beer making were taking place. This period brought the emergence of a number of commercial lager beer breweries which were largely established by German brewers who had immigrated to this country. The Germans brewed a lighter, more effervescent beer than the English ales and porters. The large-scale development of commercial lager breweries, as well as general industrialization during the last half of the nineteenth century, brought about great changes in American tastes and lifestyles with an apparent decline in home brewing. Commercially made beers were plentiful and cheap and many people were drifting away from the self-sufficient lifestyle of an agricultural society to participate in the industrial revolution in America.

It was not until the year 1920 and the implementation of the Volstead Act, which brought on the speakeasy and bathtub gin, that a resurgence in home brewing took place. By this time, the skills necessary for brewing with grains in the home had been lost. Luckily for the home brewing art, some of the breweries, which could no longer brew beer, began to manufacture malt extracts ostensibly for use in baking and other legal activities.

It is quite obvious that if all the malt extract sold during Prohibition had been used for baking, the world would have been glutted with bread. I understand that one manufacturer of malt extract facetiously included the following caution on the label of his product: "Warning, do not allow yeast to come in contact with this product. To do so will cause it to ferment into beer."

The availability of malt extract made it possible for almost anyone to brew beer in that it greatly simplified the process by eliminating the need for processing grain. Much of the beer brewed during this Prohibition period was of poor quality. There was an almost frantic demand for anything alcoholic, so many people with little knowledge of brewing gave it a try. Because of this, home brewing gained a rather bad reputation during the Prohibition period of 1920 to 1933—a reputation that we present-day brewers are still trying to live down. We've all heard of, or experienced, those semi-humorous episodes of grandpa's (or grandma's) beer bottles exploding in the basement. The "home brew" of the period is generally thought of as a murky, yeasty beverage which had but few saving graces except that in the particular time it was better to have sipped and sorrowed than to not have sipped at all.

Home brewing in this country for many years following the repeal of Prohibition was in a period of stagnation. Little of consequence happened to change the picture until the early 1970s. At this point the start of a new resurgence in home beer making occurred. Several factors have contributed to this resurgence.

The first factor seems to be a sort of backlash to what started during the last half of the nineteenth century and has accelerated through the twentieth; that is, the highly advanced industrialization and commercialization of American society. Many people have reacted to this by developing a desire to "get back to basics" and a "do it yourself" attitude.

A second factor is the standardization of beer types by the commercial brewers. Many people have drunk and appreciated different beers from Europe and elsewhere or simply wish to explore different beers outside the very limited range of those offered by the few giant breweries that are dominant in the United States. Concurrently, there is increased sensitivity on the part of consumers to the use of "additives" in commercial beer and other products. It is interesting to note at this writing that a battle royal is raging between the nation's two largest breweries over the implications of their respective advertising claims regarding the use of preservatives and other additives in their beers.

The third factor contributing to the present healthy condition of the home brewing art is the availability of brewing materials of high quality. A variety of excellent malt extracts, malted barley, hops, and yeasts are now available. Combined with this is the development of improved procedures for home brewing which can utilize the quality materials to produce the very best beers. It is to this latter purpose that this book is devoted. It is my hope that through my efforts, as well as the efforts of others, the art of home beer making can completely shed the tarnish of the Prohibition period and demonstrate the fact that beers of very high quality can be made at home.

Other Garden Way Publishing Books You Will Enjoy

From Vines to Wines . . . The Complete Guide to Growing Grapes and Making Your Own Wine, by Jeff Cox. Basing his book on a dozen years' experience, the author leads the reader through the entire procedure of winemaking. This book will appeal to the person who wants to grow grapes and make wine commercially, as well as to the wine connoisseur or casual hobbyist. 308 pages, $10.95 ISBN #0-88266-528-6

Making Homemade Wines, by Robert Cluett. This bulletin will take the mystery out of making wine — it will teach you the language of winemakers and explain what ingredients and equipment are essential, plus delicious recipes. 32 pages, $1.95 ISBN #0-88266-289-9

Making Wines, Beer and Soft Drinks, by Phyllis Hobson. Fruit juices — even clover and dandelions — make delicious wines (34 recipes). Brew your own hearty beer. Soft drinks that are wholesome. 60 pages, $3.95. ISBN #0-88266-063-2

Sweet & Hard Cider . . . Making It, Using It, and Enjoying It, by Annie Proulx and Lew Nichols. How to make, harden, distill, judge, drink, and enjoy this historic beverage, with instructions on how to select and grow cider-apple trees. 188 pages, $9.95 ISBN #0-88266-352-6

The Complete Handbook of Home Brewing, by Dave Miller. Home brewmeisters and novices will appreciate the clarity, wit, and enthusiasm of the author, a twelve-year home brewing veteran. Fifty-five recipes for all types of beers. More than a how-to book, it also makes for good reading. 256 pages. Paperback: $9.95, ISBN #0-88266-517-0; Hardcover: $19.95, ISBN #0-88266-522-7

These books are available at your bookstore or may be ordered directly from Garden Way Publishing, Dept. 8600, Schoolhouse Road, Pownal, VT 05261. Send for our free mail order catalog.

 # Glossary

Ale—Beer fermented by top-fermenting yeasts at temperatures of 55–70° F. Usually has higher hop content than lager.

Anti-oxidant—A substance added to the beer at bottling to prevent overoxidation. Ascorbic acid is most commonly used for this purpose.

Aroma—Pleasing odor in beer. Comes primarily from oils derived from hops.

Body—A sensation of fullness in the mouth. Heavy beers have more body than light beers.

Carbon dioxide—An inert gas produced during fermentation. Gives sparkle to the beer.

Cidery—An undesirable aroma and flavor in the beer resembling that of apple cider. Characteristic of Prohibition-style "home brew."

Conditioning—Establishing the proper clarity and carbonation in the beer by priming and aging in the bottle.

Dextrins—Substances produced during mashing which are not fermentable and contribute to the terminal gravity and body of the beer.

Dextrose—Corn sugar. The best all-around sugar for brewing.

Diastase—A preparation of amylase enzymes which can be added to the mash to enhance the conversion of starches to sugars.

Extract—The total solids derived from mashing malted barley and sometimes malt adjuncts such as corn or rice. Principally includes maltose, non-fermentable dextrins, and protein. These extracts in solution determine the starting gravity of the wort.

Fining—The addition of a settling agent, such as gelatin, to clarify beer.

Heading liquid—A formulation which increases head retention and produces a thick, creamy head when beer is properly carbonated.

Hops—The dried blossom of the female hop plant. When boiled with malt extract and water or mash liquor, produces desired bitterness, tangy flavor, and aroma in beer. Hops also act as a preservative in the beer.

Lager—Beer fermented by bottom-fermenting yeast at temperatures below 50° F.

Malt—Malted barley. Three main types are pale, crystal or caramel, and black.

Malt adjuncts—Various cereal grains such as corn, rice, and wheat that are added to the mash with malted barley to provide additional sources of starch and certain desired characteristics in the beer.

Malt extract—An extract obtained by mashing malt in water and concentrating into syrup or powdered form. Commercially available malt extracts (syrups) are packaged in cans and may be plain or hop flavored. Powdered or dried malt extracts (DME) are always unhopped and are usually packaged in plastic bags.

Malting—A process of germinating and drying barley grain to develop a high level of enzyme power and desired physical characteristics for use in mashes.

Maltose—The sugar derived from mashing malted barley.

Mashing—The process of cooking ground malt with water at certain temperatures for maximum enzyme activity to convert starches to fermentable sugars and dextrins, and to modify malt proteins.

Nutrients—Sources of necessary elements, mainly nitrogen and phosphorus, to keep yeast healthy throughout fermentation. A common nutrient additive is diammonium phosphate.

Oxidation—Absorption of excessive oxygen in the beer, destroying the fresh and lively taste in beer.

pH—An expression of relative acidity. Can be measured by special pH test papers. Proper pH is important to efficient mashing and good keeping qualities in the beer.

Primary fermentation—The first fermentation which is carried out in a wide-mouth container such as a crock or plastic trash can. Typically lasts from one to three days.

Priming—The addition of sugar, preferably corn sugar, to the beer just prior to bottling to promote additional fermentation in the bottle which is sufficient to properly carbonate the beer.

Racking—Transferring the beer by siphoning from one container to another to eliminate solids, mainly yeast sediments, which are left behind on the bottom of the container from which it is siphoned.

Secondary fermentation—The final part of the fermentation. This is done in a small-mouth container such as a five-gallon water bottle (carboy) which is fitted with a fermentation lock to exclude air but allow the carbon dioxide gas to escape.

Single-stage fermentation—Complete fermentation in a single container which is fitted with a fermentation lock.

Souring—Spoilage of the beer caused by bacterial contamination. Rarely occurs if proper precautions are taken regarding sanitation and protection of the beer from overexposure to air.

Sparging—Rinsing of spent grain after mash cooking by spraying with hot water to recover all of the sugars and other extracts remaining with the spent grain.

Specific gravity—The density of a liquid as compared with

that of water, the specific gravity of water being 1.000. Specific gravity is measured with a hydrometer.

Starting gravity—The specific gravity of the wort prior to the beginning of fermentation.

Steam beer—American in origin. Beer fermented with bottom-fermenting yeast at 60–70° F.

Stout—Very dark, heavy, bittersweet beer fermented with top-fermenting yeast. Has high hop content.

Stuck fermentation—Premature cessation of fermentation before the terminal gravity has been reached. Usually caused by weak yeast starter or fermentation at too low temperature.

Sucrose—Common household sugar. Derived from sugar cane or beets. Not recommended for brewing quality beers.

Sulfite—Either potassium or sodium metabisulfite. When mixed with water, produces sulfur dioxide gas. It is used as sterilizing agent for brewing equipment.

Terminal gravity—The specific gravity of the beer when fermentation is complete, that is, when all fermentable sugars have been converted to alcohol and carbon dioxide gas.

Water treatment—The addition of various substances such as salt (sodium chloride), citric acid, Burton salts, and gypsum (calcium sulfate) to adjust the hardness and pH (acidity) of the brewing water.

Wort—The bittersweet liquor resulting from mashing malt and boiling hops, or dissolving a hopped malt extract in water, or a combination of these. The liquor which is ready for the addition of yeast to be fermented into beer.

Yeast—An organism belonging to the fungus family which converts sugar to about equal parts of alcohol and carbon dioxide gas through a complex enzymatic process. Beer yeasts are classified as top- or bottom-fermenting. Top-fermenting yeasts produce ales and stouts. Bottom-fermenting yeasts produce lagers and steam beers.

Sources for Brewing Supplies

Many shopes specialize in brewing supplies. You will find them listed in your Yellow Pages under "Brewers' Equipment and Supplies" or "Winemakers' Equipment and Supplies." Consult your Yellow Pages and seek out your local supplier, who will be knowledgeable and eager to help.

If you do not have a local brewing supply shop, try writing the American Homebrewers Association, P.O. Box 287, Boulder, CO 80306-0287. Their publication, *Zymurgy*, lists many brewing suppliers in its Classified Ads section.

TABLE OF EQUIVALENTS

1 cup corn sugar (dextrose)	equals 6½ ounces by weight
1 cup can sugar (sucrose)	equals 8 ounces by weight
1 pound malt syrup	equals 0.8 pound dried malt extract
1 ounce dried leaf hops	equals 10 grams (about ⅓ ounce) powdered hops
Boiling time for powdered hops	equals approximately half the boiling time for leaf hops
1 cup malted barley	equals 4 ounces by weight
5 U.S. gallons	equals approximately 4 Imperial gallons

 Index